HAIR STYLIST VIBE

HAIR STYLIST VIBE

HOW TO GROW YOUR BUSINESS,
KEEP YOUR CLIENTS HAPPY, AND FIND
THE PERFECT SALON FOR YOU

SHIRLEY ROSE

First Edition
Printed in the United States

ISBN-13: 978-0-578-53027-7
ISBN-10: 0-578-53027-9

CONTENTS

INTRODUCTION

Being a hair stylist is an art that lets your creativity flow. This creativity will help guide you in beautifully transforming a head of hair and creating beautiful shape, movement, color, and style for your clients. Doing great hair in a consistent manner is one key to becoming a sought-after stylist.

That's where it starts, but this book is about all the other ways you can draw clients to you, make them happy, and keep them coming back as return guests. This book will give you tips on becoming a successful stylist through marketing your business, focusing on your guests, finding the right salon fit for yourself, taking care of you, and all the other "little" things you can do for your clients that will keep them happily coming back.

From the moment the client reaches out to you to the time they leave your salon; before, during, and after their service, you and your salon space will give off a vibe. How the salon looks, your personality, how you work in your space, how you speak, and your aesthetic all make up what I like to refer to as the Hair Stylist Vibe. This is your essence; it's who you are and what you bring to your career. Every one of us has our own unique vibe, and yours is what will draw clients to you. The key here is to stay true to who you are—basically, your vibe should be your true, authentic self. More often than not, clients will stay with you because they like your vibe, which many will find equally important to your talent as a stylist. All of these aspects put together are what will bring clients to you and keep them coming back time and time again.

Let this book inspire you, keep you fresh, and give you great tips on moving your career in a positive direction. Answer the questions after each chapter, do the challenge assignments, and mindfully think about how the new techniques you have learned will help you and your business thrive.

I wish you all the best on your journey to become the best stylist that you can possibly be.

Shirley

YOUR CAREER AS
A HAIRSTYLIST

––––––

Throughout this book there will be questions after each chapter for you to answer. The questions below are to get you thinking about yourself and your career as a stylist. Answer each question, and keep your answers in mind as you read through the book for ideas on where you may be able to improve and how you can make some changes and approach your salon life with positivity.

Why did you choose to become a hair stylist?

_____

_____

_____

_____

_____

Where do you see yourself in the industry in five to ten years?

_____

_____

_____

_____

_____

What are your strengths as a stylist?

_____

_____

_____

_____

_____

What are your weaknesses as a stylist?

_____

_____

_____

_____

_____

What are the things that you like about the industry?

_____

_____

_____

_____

_____

What are the things that you dislike about the industry?

_____

_____

_____

_____

_____

Do you currently have a marketing strategy?

_____

_____

_____

_____

_____

Do you have a self-care regimen? If yes, what is it?

_____

_____

_____

_____

_____

If no, what types of things would you like to start doing to take care of yourself?

_____

_____

_____

_____

What do you love doing the most as a stylist?

_____

_____

_____

_____

_____

Do you have particular services that you would like to focus on?

_____

_____

_____

_____

_____

Are you happy at your current salon?

_____

_____

_____

_____

_____

CHAPTER 1

GET YOUR NAME OUT THERE

———

We all would love to have an infinitely large clientele that just shows up at our door. The reality of this business, however, is that getting new clients does not come easily; it's something you'll have to work on as much as possible. You need to come up with ways to get their attention, pull them in, and then give them exceptional service and attention to detail. Luckily for you, there are a lot of ways to attract new guests, and just as many ways to retain them.

Marketing yourself is something you should be doing every chance you get. Really put yourself out there, because the more effort you put in, the greater your chances of success. Attracting new clients will take a lot of hard work, but once you figure out what works for you, it will become easier, and you may actually enjoy the challenge. From printed materials and digital marketing to special events and client referrals, there are countless ways to spread the word about your business and to highlight your own Hair Stylist Vibe.

BUSINESS CARDS

Having well-thought-out business cards that beautifully fit your aesthetic will really make you stand out. Make sure your business cards include your name; the salon's name, address, and phone number (and/or your cell phone number); and any other useful information. Keep your business cards with you and hand them out to people you meet. Grocery store lines, banks, restaurants, the gym, and doctor's and dentist's offices are all great places to casually strike up a conversation with someone. Get in the habit of chatting with people you don't know. A good conversation starter might be something to do with their hair—or if they happen to mention liking your hair (because of course it always looks fabulous), that's your in! Tell them you're a stylist and give them a card. I was recently chatting with a woman while we were both getting our cars' oil changed. When I told her I was a stylist and had my own salon, she asked me for my information, and I was very glad I had my cards with me. These conversations can happen just about anywhere, as long as you're willing to talk with people, let them know what you do, and put yourself out there.

SALON MENU

A salon menu is another great way to let people know what you do and how to find you. Again, the look of your menu should fit your personal vibe and your salon's style. Have these on hand to give out to prospective clients, and give them to your existing clients, too, so they will know all the services that you offer. Make sure to include the salon's name, your name and a short bio, the salon's address and phone number or your cell phone number, the salon's website and Instagram, Twitter, Facebook, or other social media handles, your hours, and a list of your services. You can add prices if you like, adding a note at the bottom that reads "Prices subject to change." Add thoughtful and enticing details about what your services entail. For instance, instead of writing "shampoo," "cut," and "style," which sounds a bit ordinary, you could write:

- Relaxing wash: Get pampered and feel relaxed with our luxurious shampoo.
- Precision haircut: We tailor our haircuts to suit you and bring out your features beautifully.
- Finishing touches: Let us style your hair for you and show you how to maintain your gorgeous look at home.

The services are the same, but the wording makes your salon sound more luxurious.

REFERRAL PROGRAM

How about doing a referral program? There are so many options. Have some beautiful postcard-sized cards made up for your guests. Make them quite large so they won't be discarded easily. Keep the referral part simple. You could do a percentage off a haircut for the new guest, and give your existing client who did the referral a percentage off as well. This gets new people in the door and encourages your existing clients to spread the word about you, since they will love the discount as well. Wait until the new client's second appointment, then give them a few referral cards too. Talk to every single client that sits in your chair about how your program works. Also, post a picture of the referral card on all of your social media accounts and your website. This kind of program can quickly get more people in to see you. I've also seen some salons do a punch card, where after so many services you get a free haircut. Or try another variation, like when your client sends you a certain amount of referrals, that client gets a free service of their choosing. These are just a few ideas to get you started, but you can have success with any nice incentive that will get your clients excited to refer their family, friends, or coworkers to you.

BUSINESS LOGO

Having a well-thought-out logo is a great way to be recognized and help brand your business. Come up with a design that showcases who you are, what you do, and your personal vibe. This could include your name or the name of the salon that you work in. Logos are great for business cards, salon menus, referral cards, and your website, and your logo should appear on every one of your social media accounts. Make sure the logo is one that your clients will instantly recognize and that will really pique their interest when it pops up on their social media feeds. Branding yourself this way will get you noticed and hopefully result in better engagement on your posts. To create your logo, ideally consult with a graphic designer. You should choose the best designer for you based on their portfolio, whether the two of you have the same vision, and whether you feel they are capable of doing the design you want.

Getting out in the world and being seen can have a big effect on your business. Try having a few T-shirts made with the name of your salon on them. Make sure that you put your logo on them, too. This is a great conversation starter and a simple step that can definitely boost your business. Another idea is to have decals made for your vehicle, again, making sure that your logo is prominently displayed.

LOCAL BUSINESS CONNECTIONS

Do you know someone who works in a store or an office? Give those people your referral cards or menus to hand out. Have them put some out in a break room or at the front desk. Drop off your business cards at a local senior center. If you know a local teacher, they can put them in school mailboxes for other teachers. If you have restaurants in your area, ask if you could leave some business cards at their front entrance. Some smaller local restaurants may even have a bulletin board where you can put up a few cards or menus. A nearby hotel that hosts gatherings, weddings, or holiday parties would be a fantastic place to have your menu on display. Many of their guests may be visiting from out of town and be in need of these services while they are in your area. Realtors are another great group to connect with—since they come into contact with new people who are just moving into your area, ask if they could slip your menu into their welcome-home packets, and in return, take some of their business cards to hand out to your clients who may be in need of their service. The art of working together with your community just makes good business sense. There are so many ways of getting to know your local businesses so that you can work together to build connections and watch your businesses thrive.

When you put yourself out there and get noticed, it will impact your career in a very positive way. Check in your area for small business fairs, local groups or organizations having meet-and-greets, and flea markets or craft fairs that are looking for people to rent a booth. Why not sign up for one of these events to get you and your salon noticed? Make sure you have a large banner made up with your logo on it, and bring all of your salon's promotional materials, including pictures of your stunning creations. Are you a bridal stylist? If so, attending a bridal expo can provide great exposure for you and is a perfect place to show off what you can do. Get a booth and decorate it to stand out and be noticed. Be sure to bring picture samples of your work, along with your brochures, menus, and cards.

PRINTING FOR YOUR BUSINESS

Having all of your necessary menus and business cards made up may sound like it will cost a fortune. However, if you take some time to shop comparatively, it may be less expensive than you think. You may want to research your options online and then also visit directly with your local printing companies. When you do both and compare, you will have more choices, and in a local shop you will be able to view their work. Do some homework to determine the right fit for you and decide who you'd like to do business with. Most printing companies have designers who can help you get exactly the look that you want, or you can go with their standard templates. You will want to go with the company that can finish the order in a timely manner and has the skill to do exactly what you need at a fair price. Some of these companies may offer discounts on larger orders, so be sure to ask! Volume discounts can be a great deal, especially if you will be needing business cards, banners, referral cards, and salon menus.

MARKETING A SALON GIVEAWAY

Doing a giveaway is a way to focus on the salon that will get lots of attention from your clients and potential new clients. You can choose to give away a single gift or a combination of items. For a larger combination, first select a beautiful gift bag or basket. Fill it up with carefully chosen hair products, such as shampoo, conditioner, hair spray, gel, mousse, or dry shampoo. Add some hair accessories, like decorative clips, headbands, a brush, or a comb. You could also add a curling iron or a straightener if those would be in your budget. Adding a gift certificate for a salon service is nice, because if a new client wins you'll have the opportunity to retain that client, and if an existing client wins they will be very grateful and will want to get the word out about your fabulous, giving salon.

A giveaway works best if posted to social media. Post a picture on your salon's and stylists' pages of what you're giving away. Make sure it is attention-grabbing—this is where choosing the perfect gift bag or basket comes in. What you want to do next is to ask your followers to like, comment on, and share the post. When they do this, they will automatically be entered to win. Two or three weeks is a good amount of time to keep the post going and then pick a winner. This will definitely get some interest and also get your name and the salon's name out into the world.

When you pick the winner, be sure to post that as well. If possible get a picture of the prize winner with their swag and post away. The more people that see the posts, the more attention your salon will receive. If you happen to do another giveaway, anyone that saw the happy recipient of the previous prize will definitely want to participate.

SIDEWALK SIGN

Whether your salon is in a strip mall, office suite, or stand-alone building, try using a sidewalk display board to attract the attention of people passing by. (Note that you may need special approval first from your building management, city, or town.) Write the name of your salon at the top, then you can write whatever you think will attract the most attention. Write about a special offer or exclusive services, or write something funny to get noticed. Adding balloons will get even more eyes on your board. You may be surprised by how many people will stop in and say, "I never knew you were here!"

SOCIAL MEDIA

Social media is where you will build and nurture relationships with people. For this reason, it's best to keep your social media business pages professional and authentic. Try to be on as many social media sites as you can (for example, Facebook, Instagram, Twitter, and LinkedIn), as this will allow more people to get to know you and see what you can do. Post your gorgeous content frequently to get more attention. You may want to put yourself on a schedule to post at a certain time of the day and on certain days of the week, and your followers will then look forward to seeing each day's post. In addition to showing your work through beautiful photos or captivating videos, another great way to see more engagement is to have your followers take part in a poll or to ask a question. For example, if you are in the process of designing a new logo for your business, show your followers a few different designs that you have chosen and have them pick which one they like. Then when the final decision is made, you can post the finished product, and make sure to thank everyone for their input. Doing something like this will encourage people to make a choice, then they will want to see the finished product. Most people like to be part of a decision-making process, so let them.

VIDEO

Video is a wonderful tool to use on your social media sites and your website. Videos have become wildly popular, and for good reason. There is so much good content to share with potential clients, and sharing it will get you out there and noticed. If you choose to post videos, make sure you stay professional, but have fun with it. Explain what you are doing, so your audience will have a clear understanding from start to finish. Also, try to keep them on the shorter side or your audience may lose interest. Some content that will help you get your name out there:

- Take a video of your salon while it is bustling with stylists and their guests.
- Make a how-to video. Show how to do a simple night-out hairstyle, braid, or updo.
- Create a video showing your followers how to solve their hair problems. For example, show how to use product to get more fullness for fine hair, or how to smooth curly or unruly hair, or show men how to apply gel, pomade, styling cream, or clay.
- Find a model to help demonstrate techniques your followers can try at home, such as how to use dry shampoo, how to use heat-protecting spray while using a straightener, or how to use spray shine.

SOCIAL MEDIA MANAGER

For anyone who struggles with marketing themselves on social media (not an easy thing to master), you may want to outsource to a social media manager. Depending on what you are trying to achieve, this person can share your content or create it for you. They will create well-thought-out ads to target audiences on your social media platforms. They will also respond to comments on the posts or videos. Having someone knowledgeable to tackle this for you on all of your social media sites will give you a big advantage in gaining much-needed visibility on your online platforms. The cost of this service varies depending on how many platforms they will be managing, whether they are creating content or posting yours, the cost of the ads you choose to purchase, and the length of time that you need them.

WOWING WITH YOUR WEBSITE

Your website can be your most successful way of bringing clients to you and is a vital part of your business. Anyone looking for your services online will find you first through your website, and will likely decide within a few minutes whether you are the chosen one. This is why you need to have a very well-designed site that will make you stand out to your potential clients. Design your site without too many confusing or complicated links. Be simplistic. You want your potential clients to stay on your website, not get frustrated because they aren't sure how to navigate it and leave. Always keep your salon aesthetic in mind when picking colors and fonts to use. Must haves for your website include your salon's logo, address, hours of operation, location (including a map); how to contact you, including a call to action button and phone number; services offered (prices optional); and online booking information. To let potential clients know who you are and what you do, make your site a bit more personal by putting up a picture of each stylist with a short bio detailing their expertise, credentials, and the story of how they got to be where they are, doing what they love. Adding photos of your salon will give potential clients a glimpse into the salon before they come in. This is important for those somewhat shy or nervous first-time clients who may need a visual before they make an appointment to feel comfortable about visiting your salon. Lastly, adding quality photos of the work you do and updating those photos often will show your future guests what you are capable of. Clients will be drawn to you through your website, and essentially it is an extension of who you are and what your salon stands for. So go above and beyond when designing it.

FIND A GREAT WEB DESIGNER

Finding someone to design your website may take a little work on your part, unless you happen to already know someone with website design experience who can help you out. If not, there are various ways of finding a web designer to work with:

- Ask the business that prints out your business cards or referral cards if they also do web design.
- Ask for recommendations on Facebook. Some of your friends may know of a good web designer, or may even be one themselves.
- Go online and search for web designers in your area, making sure to read the reviews about their performance. Meet with a few of them to get a sense of whether you would be comfortable working with them and to see their work and capabilities.

ADVERTISING

There are many ways to promote your business through both digital and more traditional advertising. Occasionally, you could pay for a Facebook ad or to boost a post. You will be able to pick who can see the content based on their location, age group, and gender. You can also pay to advertise in a local newspaper. Direct mail through the post office can be a great tool to use for promotions and offerings to people nearby. Or make up eye-catching flyers that you can hand out to potential clients or local businesses. Put yourself in the shoes of a would-be client, and think about what would attract you to a business. What could that business offer that you couldn't refuse? Would they offer a service that no one else offers? Make the answers to these questions part of your promotion and marketing.

As stylists we all offer something that is unique and special. Think about what that is for you and showcase it. Do you specialize in clipper cutting, fashion hair color, smoothing treatments, updos, or makeup application? Whatever makes you stand out, that is what you need to feature through advertising. Otherwise, how is anyone to know what your special talent is and where to find you?

CLIENT REVIEWS

Now that you understand the importance of getting yourself online and you have gotten on as many sites as you can find, it's time to ask your clients to give you some online reviews. Because we know that future clients are checking you out online and will make a decision about whether or not to book with you based on those reviews, this is an important aspect of your online presence. Ask your clients to Google your salon name (or find you through any other search site they may use) and leave a review. It's that simple! Most of your clients will be very happy to do this for you, as they know it will help you, so ask today!

SMALL-BUSINESS SATURDAY

In the United States, the Saturday after Thanksgiving is "small-business Saturday," and if you own your own business or work in a locally-owned salon, it's your day to shine. Because this weekend typically starts the holiday shopping season, it's the perfect time for you or your salon to advertise specials, promotions, and possibly discounts for this very special day of recognition on social media, in the salon, on a sidewalk display board, and more. Some ideas include offering delicious food or seasonal beverages in the salon, advertising holiday gift ideas and gift card sales, and doing product demos. Ask your Product Representative for some product samples that you can give out to guests—this is a nice way for your clients to try a product, love it, and then know where to come back and buy it. Do you know someone that sells homemade candy, candles, jewelry, or hair accessories? You could invite them to your salon to set up a table. Your clients will love the shopping experience, and the seller will enjoy the exposure that being in your salon will offer.

HOLIDAY AND
SPECIAL-OCCASION IDEAS

Make the most of every holiday and special occasion you can think of! Here are a few ideas for holiday promotions that you can post on social media, put up on your website, and advertise on flyers in-salon to keep your happy clients coming back and draw new clients who love some perks:

- Mother's and Father's Day can be celebrated throughout May or June, and these holidays are a great time to show all your Mom and Dad clients some love. Treat them to a service special, a delicious treat, or a raffle for a Mother's or Father's Day basket.

- Birthday specials are a nice way to acknowledge your client's special day. You could offer your guest a percentage off a new service that they have never tried before during their birth month. This is a win-win, because the client gets to try a new service, and they may love it and book that service with you again for a future appointment. You can also choose something special to showcase during your own birth month. I ran a scalp massage special during my birth month and it really got a lot of interest.

- Black Friday is another day to amp up your product and gift card sales. People love to try new things, so why not demonstrate how to use all of your wonderful products? For example, advertise and perhaps have an in-salon demonstration of a new curling iron or straightening iron, show clients how to wear cute headbands, or demonstrate how they can make their hair shimmer using spray shine. Make sure you have plenty of product on hand to sell.

- Your salon anniversary can be a very fun and uplifting time—and truly, it does not matter if your salon has been open for one year or ten! There is a certain pride in knowing you are part of a salon that has endured, and having an anniversary celebration is a great reminder of this. Host a party with balloons and a cake. Make every client aware of the bash by posting on social media and hanging a flyer in your salon. This will be a thoughtful and well-deserved celebration for both stylists and clients.

- Earth Day is the time to go green. As a gift to your guests you could give out Happy Earth Day flowering seed packets or small plants. In the salon, you can make a difference by asking guests to bring in reusable water bottles and coffee mugs for their salon drinks, using less water, unplugging curling and straightening irons when not in use, going bagless or reusing gift bags for product purchases, dimming the salon lights or turning them off (as long as you have enough light from outdoors filtering in), and getting a recycling bin (if you don't already have one). This is simple to execute . . . and in return, we all get a cleaner Earth!

This chapter is full of ideas to market yourself and get your name out there. Whether you are a new stylist, or you've been in business for a while but haven't put much effort into promoting yourself, the time is now! Be brave and put yourself out there to be seen. How are new clients supposed to find you, if you are hidden? How are they to know what your true magic is? Try the marketing ideas in this chapter to see what works for you. Success will come when you are consistently trying new things to see what works.

QUESTION

When you are looking for a particular service provider, such as a massage therapist, nail artist, or esthetician, how do you go about finding the right one? Write down your answers, then use the same methods to promote your own business.

_____

_____

_____

_____

_____

TIME TO REFLECT AND
TAKE THE CHALLENGE

In this chapter you learned how to get your name out into the world. For the next five days, do one thing each day that will let people know who you are, what you do, and where to find you. Be brave and go outside of your comfort zone. Use the examples in this chapter or come up with your own ideas to bring in new business.

_____

_____

_____

_____

_____

CHAPTER 2

FOCUS ON YOUR GUEST

Getting the word out and getting new clients in the door is the first step in building your business, but even more important is making sure those clients have a positive experience so that they will return time and time again. When your client enters the salon, your focus should be on them. Greet them, sit with them for a little chat and hair consultation, offer a drink or snack, then get started. Your guest wants to feel important and doted on. Doing this will give them a deep rooted feeling that they are in the right salon with the best stylist.

As a stylist, you have the ability to make your clients' time with you in the salon very enjoyable, so that over time they will really begin looking forward to their appointments with you. Their salon time will have an ease to it that will give them comfort, allowing them to open up to you about themselves and enjoy the conversations that you will have with them.

LISTEN AND BE POSITIVE

Listening is key! People like to talk about themselves, and that's okay—let them. Let your clients talk about their hair, their lives, or the kind of day they are having. You want them to feel comfortable and for the conversation to flow organically. Try to keep things positive, and don't start talking negatively about all the terrible stuff happening in your life. You may lose clients if you do this.

If the conversation starts to become unpleasant, gently switch it back to a positive. Negative conversation can be stressful for you and your guest. Keeping things upbeat will give your guests the type of relaxing service that they are looking for.

When you get to know your clients, you can focus on them and truly care about their wants and needs. These are the things that will draw them to you and keep them returning. Treating each of them in a warm and friendly manner and being respectful of their needs and their time will completely reinforce to your guests that they are in good hands.

SLIGHT DISTRACTIONS

We all know that working in a salon comes with its fair share of distractions. For instance, while you're working on a guest a coworker may talk to you or ask a question, another guest may start up a conversation, a product representative may pop in, or a new client may walk in. These interruptions are more than likely short in duration. What is key here is to excuse yourself from your guest and do whatever needs to be done in a timely manner, then go back to focusing on the person sitting in your chair. This will show your client how attentive you are and that you understand their time is important.

Unlike the slight distractions I just spoke of, you should always refrain from talking on your phone while servicing a guest. The only exceptions would be for a truly important call or an emergency. I know of stylists that will wear a headset and carry on full conversations while working. This is not professional, nor is it fair to your guests. Also, if you do have to take a personal call, try to find an area of seclusion in the salon or go outdoors. Your clients and coworkers really don't need to hear your private conversation, as this could make anyone within earshot of you feel uncomfortable. A better idea would be to leave your phone in the back room, where you can periodically go and check it.

EARLY CLIENTS

Sometimes clients will show up early for their appointments. This is completely fine and can actually help you, since a late guest can really mess up your schedule.

But if you are still servicing your previous client, this is where your focus needs to remain. Most guests understand this and will sit and wait for their turn. Some clients, though, may want to start chatting with you. What to do? First, let them know that you will be with them shortly and that they can take a seat in the reception area. Offer them a snack and beverage while they wait. Then you can get back to your guest and finish up with them.

MAINTAIN FOCUS

Even when working in a larger-scale salon, where there are many clients being serviced at one time, stay on task with your guest. As hard as this may seem at times, it is a necessary ingredient to keeping the person in your chair happy. I guarantee the person sitting in your chair won't appreciate it if you are more interested in the client next to you and what they are doing with their hair, or are having long conversations with another stylist. There is nothing wrong with having light and friendly conversation with others around you, but you should try to keep the conversations with others to a minimum if they are interfering with the time you have with *your* guest.

Having worked in large salons myself, I know all too well the struggles of keeping fully focused. When there are always commotions going on, blow dryers running, other stylists conversing, and phones ringing, at times it can seem impossible to stay fully focused. If this happens to you, you need to stay mindfully and purposefully devoted to your work, while blocking out the background hum. This will take some practice; however, the more you stay aligned to your client and block out all other things, the more fully focused and committed you become to them and all the details of their appointment.

CHOOSE THE RIGHT SALON FOR YOU

Maybe you enjoy working in a large salon filled with people having lively conversations and a spirited commotion. Being in this type of salon has many benefits. If you ever have a question, you have plenty of experienced stylists to help you problem solve. When you are away from the salon for any length of time, there will be someone your clients can see while you're out. When you need your own hair done, you'll have your choice of stylists. There can be a nice camaraderie that is felt while working in a larger salon. If this atmosphere makes you happy and you can remain focused on your guest within it, then you have found the right place.

Perhaps you are more in favor of a quiet, subdued salon with one-on-one attention. This type of salon has many benefits of its own. You will have an easier time focusing on your guest with fewer people around—in fact, it may just be the two of you. You will be able to offer more personal services in peace, and there won't be any interruptions. You and your guest will be able to relax and speak freely without being concerned about who may overhear. If you feel your focus would be better in a smaller setting, then you may be better suited for a petite salon, a salon suite, a mobile salon, or an at-home salon.

This is a very personal decision, and only you know what is best, so follow your heart and what you feel is right. Wherever you end up, just make sure that you are happy in that environment and can fully focus on your priority: your guest.

QUESTION

While you are working on a client, pay attention to your focus. Is it fixed on your client, or is your mind wandering? Are you paying attention to other conversations going on around you? What can you do to remain focused on your guest?

_____

_____

_____

_____

_____

TIME TO REFLECT AND
TAKE THE CHALLENGE

When you are at the salon servicing a guest, make a mental note of the situations that occur that make you lose your focus. Create a list of these triggers. For the next seven days, reread the list before work. Remember what you wrote, and when these triggers arise, try to retrain your focus to stay solely on your guest.

_____

_____

_____

_____

_____

CHAPTER 3

SELF-CARE FOR THE STYLIST

Having a career as a stylist is a great joy! You get to work with fabulous clients and help them look and feel their best. Doing so, however, can be emotionally and physically draining on you, since you'll be working long hours on your feet and always having to be at your best. This is why taking care of yourself is extremely important—not only for your well-being (and that of your family) but for the well-being of your clients. The list that follows includes some self-care tips to help you make every day a beautiful fresh start.

1. Getting a good night's sleep is essential for your well-being and your ability to function. To ensure a restful sleep, you may want to maintain a routine before bed, which could include taking a warm

bath or shower, moisturizing your face, drinking a little water, putting on comfortable sleep clothes, reading, listening to music, or watching a show. Make sure your bedroom is dark and on the cooler side. Consider going "screenless" one to two hours before bed—this will help you disconnect and un-plug, aid in relaxation, and give your mind a rest.

2. During the evening hours, prepare for the next day in order to make your mornings as easy as possible. Watch the weather for the next day and set out your clothes and shoes. Figure out what you will have for breakfast, then pack your lunch and snacks for the day. Lastly, take the time to pack a bag with every-thing you will need for your day at the salon. Doing these things will really help you to relax and keep the chaos to a minimum in the morning.

3. Having a good breakfast and having healthy food at the salon is extremely important to your well-being. This will give you energy and keep you go-ing. While at the salon, take breaks to sit down and eat! No one wants to start feeling light-headed or dizzy, and believe me, your clients pay attention and will know if you're feeling "off." Make sure to bring snacks that you can graze on throughout the day. Fruit, eggs, cheese, raw vegetables and dip,

nuts, granola bars, trail mix, yogurt, and smoothies are all good on-the-go choices. Try to avoid unhealthy, sugary, or high-fat foods. These will give you a quick boost, only to make you feel sluggish later on. Always have water, juice, or smoothies with you and make sure to drink up. A little tip that I learned is to put cut-up fruit, such as oranges, lemons, limes, grapes, kiwis, and strawberries, at the bottom of a take-along cup and fill with water. You can keep filling the cup throughout the day to draw all the juice and nutrients from the fruit while staying hydrated. At the end of the day, eat the fruit. This is a win-win: you stay hydrated all day long, and get to enjoy the delicious fruit.

4. Before you leave for work in the morning, take a few minutes at home to prepare for your day. Close your eyes and do a little meditation or mindful thinking, keeping your thoughts peaceful. The idea is to not let any negative thoughts come into your mind. Negative energy will only make you feel sluggish and not capable of your best work. This may be a good time to think about your salon life and mentally prepare yourself for a wonderful workday.

5. Mornings can also be a nice time to do some stretches, go for a walk or run, or if you are really

motivated, hit the gym. I realize mornings can be a crazy time, between getting ready for work, taking the dog out, and getting your kids ready for school, but even just doing a few stretches is better than nothing. Doing these things will help keep you fit and get your mind and body ready for the workday.

6. Make sure to wear comfortable shoes. I know this seems like a no-brainer, but sometimes we all need a gentle reminder. As a stylist, you spend most days on your feet. It is imperative for your long-term health that you wear supportive shoes. The first step would be to go to a shoe store that has good quality footwear and have your feet measured. If you haven't done this in a long time, you may be surprised at what size you actually are. Then you want to try on the shoes that will give you the most support and have a nice thick cushion. There are lots of shoes and sneakers to choose from that will give you the style and comfort you need. Manufacturers have come a long way with fashionable comfort footwear. Try to avoid wearing high heels, high heeled boots, or completely flat shoes, which have no support at all, to work. In the long run, your feet and back will thank you!

7. For the comfort of your feet, legs, and back, I would highly recommend getting an anti-fatigue

padded floor mat to stand on while at work. If the salon you work at does not have them, perhaps you could suggest to the manager or owner that they supply these for you and your coworkers. Having a mat will make those long periods of time on your feet more manageable.

8. Always dress the part. How you dress says a lot about your style, personality, and how you appear to the world. Dress for the career you want, and make sure you're putting effort into what you wear. Your clothing choices have a huge impact on how you feel and your confidence level. Dressing smartly gives you a boost, but it doesn't have to mean spending a fortune on your wardrobe. (And due to the fact that you will get hair, bleach, and color on your clothes, you shouldn't!) Try shopping at secondhand or thrift stores—these are fabulous stores filled with stylish clothes at reasonable prices. Invest in a stylist apron. These can be very stylish, have amazing pockets for all your "stylist stuff," and will save your wardrobe from color and bleach. Some salons have uniforms or a dress code that needs to be followed. This can work in your favor, since you won't ruin your wardrobe, and you can usually spruce things up with jewelry, cute hair accents, and a nice pair of comfortable shoes.

9. Speaking of hair . . . what about yours? As stylists we are notorious for being behind the chair so much that we neglect being in it! Has it been a while since you had a good cut, highlights, or a root touch-up? Keeping up with your hair is important, and you need to make time for it. Maybe it's time for a new style? How about a new color? Not only will it give you a boost, but it may inspire your clients to change up their hair as well.

10. Writing in a journal can be very helpful and fun. I personally like to write about all the positives in my personal and professional life. I write about things I want to do, places to go, new products to try, new suggestions for my clients, and so many other things. You could write about your vacation plans and upcoming events, or make lists of podcasts you want to listen to, new product lines to try, ideas for getting organized, or classes you would like to take. Why not pick up a journal today and start writing?

11. Listen to inspirational podcasts while you are heading into the salon. This is such a positive tool to use for guidance on your personal and professional growth and development. The great thing is there is no effort on your part; all you do is sit back, listen, and learn. Podcasts can be extremely

motivational and will teach, give tips, and inspire. Some of my favorites are about hair, marketing, and writing, but whatever inspires you, I'm sure there is a podcast for that.

12. Be prompt. It's a good idea to arrive at the salon at least fifteen to twenty minutes early. This will afford you the time to set up your station, tidy up, fold towels, get organized, make sure you have everything you need, and look over your notes for the clients that day in a relaxed manner. For your own peace of mind (and for the sake of your guests), try to not be late. Rushing in at the last minute is not good for you or your client.

13. Take a class. It doesn't have to be about hair (although those are great too)—there are lots of classes that will move your career along. For instance, take a design class and learn to create beautiful business cards or flyers, or try a marketing class that will show you how to advertise and be more accessible on social media. Join a photography class to learn how to take amazing pictures of clients, or a business class if you ever plan on going independent or opening up your own salon. All of these would be beneficial to you as a stylist or salon owner, and learning new ideas will inspire you to do really great things. Never stop learning!

14. Pamper yourself. As a stylist, you are used to giving wonderful and relaxing services. But what about you? Don't you deserve to get pampered too? Of course you do! Get a relaxing massage. Have the massage therapist focus on the parts that need a little TLC. I occasionally enjoy a foot massage or a deep tissue massage for my back, arms, and shoulders. These are generally the parts of our bodies that take a beating. Get your nails done with a hand massage, or go for a relaxing facial. Not only is having a service done a nice treat, it's also a great way to get tips on how to treat your guests.

    Personally, when I have a service done, I like to visit a small local business. I like the fact that I am helping a smaller establishment meet their goals, and I enjoy that one-on-one attention. Due to the fact that I'm a small business owner myself, I understand the importance of frequenting these smaller shops.

15. Take time off. Visit the ocean or a lake, go for a bike ride or hike, go shopping, take up a craft or hobby, visit an amusement park or botanical garden, enjoy a wine tasting or a new restaurant, or see a play. Do whatever makes you happy and gets you away for a while. We all need to take a break every now and then, even if it's just for a day or two. When you do

this something amazing happens: you will go back to the salon fresh and renewed.

16. While you are out and about, observe others for inspiration. For instance, I can be at a movie theater and I tend to look at people's hair. Whether it's the moviegoers or the stars on the screen, I take it all in and then I can adapt those new ideas to my guests. A sidewalk cafe on a busy street is a wonderful place to sit, look at the scenery, and people watch. Ideas are everywhere. One of my favorite things to do is to visit an art museum. I like to sit and look deeply at the paintings, focusing on the colors, textures, and patterns. I take pictures, if the museum allows, so that later on I can really study them, and I use the paintings to get inspiration for a new wall color, a pattern for curtains or rugs, ideas for artwork, or even an idea for a new vase or sculpture. Wherever your time off takes you, let it inspire and relax you.

17. Join or create a group on social media. I started a Salon Decorating group, for example, which has really made me happy and helped me to feel connected to like-minded members. My group is for stylists and owners who enjoy discussing, posting pictures of, and giving and getting advice on salon style, decor,

and design. The group that you join can be focused on whatever excites you—and if you can't find one, how about starting your own group? Making a group will keep you associated with people who care about the things you do. Not sure what it is that you are passionate about? Pay attention to the things you talk about a lot, that get you thinking and that make you feel happy. Groups can make you feel connected to others who have similar interests and can be a great place to give and get advice.

18. Read a great book. Reading is a nice way to learn new things and keep you excited about your career. There are lots of books that relate to our business that you can learn and grow from. Whether you'd like an instructional book about hairstyles, marketing, photography, business management, or how to open up your own salon, there are so many to choose from. Audio books are nice since you can listen while driving to and from the salon or while you're out running errands. Or choose a magazine—hair and makeup magazines are a great way to keep current with styles and trends.

19. Write a great book. Maybe you have an idea for a book that you have been thinking about. Writing is so good for your mind and spirit, it's a great

vocabulary and conversation builder, it's relaxing, it keeps your mind sharp, and it can be very cathartic. If you have ever thought of writing a blog, a book, poetry, or a memoir, do it! There are so many benefits and you have nothing to lose.

20. Do yourself a very big favor and work fewer hours a day. Sounds funny, right? But how tired you feel while you are servicing your clients will definitely show in your work. If you are overdoing it and working way too many hours, your last few clients of the day will suffer (and so will you). You may rush through them, make preventable mistakes, and possibly lose them. Try working fewer hours in a day, but working an extra day, to spread out your workload and allow yourself to take your time with your clients. You will be less tired and they will feel less rushed.

21. See a therapist. This is just a good and healthy thing to do. When clients come in to see you, they generally like to talk about their lives and what's happened since their last appointment. Having these conversations with you can be very helpful for your clients, but what about you? You deserve (and need) the chance to get things off your mind and take in some good advice, but the time for you to vent is not while you have a client in your chair. Your

clients should not hear about all the bad things that you have going on in your life. You should have a therapist for that. Your guests have come into the salon to be pampered, to feel uplifted, and to speak freely; you should respectfully accept that and never burden them with your problems.

22. Purposefully slow yourself down, with clients and life! Take a deep breath and give yourself time and space. You are no use to anyone if you are constantly on the go, running late and rushing around. Always give yourself plenty of time to get to where you need to be. It's better to be early so you can take a breath and not feel like you are living life frantically.

23. Come up with some positive affirmations to keep yourself feeling good throughout the day. An affirmation can be a word or a sentence that has meaning to you and has a calming effect on you. Think of something meaningful and use it as your guide whenever needed. Repeat it throughout the day while in traffic, waiting in a long line, or dealing with a difficult situation.

24. Try taking a more minimalist approach to your salon life. Buy only what you absolutely need to perform your job to the best of your ability. As a stylist,

you are constantly inundated with the latest and greatest hair products, appliances, and gadgets, but you don't necessarily need every new product that comes out on the market. Try to limit your spending to the supplies that you know will help you achieve your goals. Doing this will help curb your spending, keep more money in the bank, and simplify your salon life. Having too much stuff lying around makes it hard to find things when they're needed, makes it harder to keep the salon clean, and just doesn't look nice.

25. Get moving and keep fit! When you exercise, you will feel healthier, stronger, and more awake, which is an absolute must for this career. Try a class at the local gym, go for hikes, try yoga, ride a bike, or go for a walk. Being active is great for your cardiovascular health and endurance, increases blood flow, improves flexibility, builds muscle, leads to better posture . . . the list of benefits goes on and on!

26. Think of yourself as a flourishing stylist and become one. When you feel confident, it shows, and clients will see it and gravitate to you. This doesn't mean that you act as though you're better than anyone else—it means you value yourself, and when you do that, others will too.

27. Remember that it's okay to say "no." Overextending yourself by saying yes to everything that is asked of you does not do you or anyone else any good. If you happen to be one of those people who has a hard time saying no, that means you're a person who needs to say it more often. For your own sanity, do yourself a favor and only say yes when you truly mean it. Doing this will free up your schedule to do the things that you actually want to do.

28. Be prepared for the unexpected. Family emergencies, surgeries, and other major life events can be very trying for many reasons—not the least of which is the effect they can have on your work life. If you need surgery, for example, one of the many things that will need your consideration is who will look after your clients while you are away. Come up with a plan for who will handle your clients' appointments while you are out. Ideally you would want someone in your salon—preferably a stylist who is well-known to your guests—to take over your clients until you return. Give that person all of your guests' details, including their names, telephone numbers, and details on their haircuts, color applications, and prices. Knowing that your clients will be in good hands and their service will be seamless will give you peace of mind. Make sure to also give your guests the name, number,

and any booking information of the stylist who will be covering for you. If you know way ahead of time about the dates you'll be out, you can pre-book your guests before you leave and then book them in for when you return. If you'll be returning from a surgery, childbirth, or other health-related absence, make sure you give yourself plenty of time to heal—your body will need to rest, and rushing back to work too soon could work against you and ultimately lengthen your recovery. This is especially important in this profession, since we mostly stand and are very hands-on and active. Try to keep your appointment book light for the first week or two to allow yourself to transition back to work with ease. This may feel impossible to do, since your clients will be missing you and want to see you as soon as they can, but you absolutely need to stick to a manageable schedule, taking your time to book your clients in with ease.

29. Invest in yourself. Buy the nice clothes that will make you feel confident, get the facial or massage, go on that much-needed vacation, splurge on the better-quality equipment, or buy that nice camera or ring light to take the best possible pictures you can take. All of these nice things that you do for yourself will lift your spirits, keep you excited about our industry, and make you more sought after as a stylist.

QUESTION

Can you name a few small changes you can make at home or in the salon that would make your life a bit easier?

_____

_____

_____

_____

_____

_____

_____

TIME TO REFLECT AND
TAKE THE CHALLENGE

In this chapter you learned how to take care of you! In the space provided below, make a list of things you can do to pamper yourself that will make you feel refreshed. Then, one by one, do them and check them off your list.

_____

_____

_____

_____

_____

_____

CHAPTER 4

THE SALON EXPERIENCE: THE THREE S'S

———

First impressions mean everything, and for your salon, that means the "three S's": Sight, Scent, and Sound. How your salon looks, smells, and what your guests hear when they enter all play a large role in the overall vibe. Keep in mind the salon experience is what will entice your guests to return.

SIGHT

When a guest walks into your salon, the first thing they will do is to look around and observe. This is why it is so important that your salon be nicely decorated, clutter-free, clean, and in good repair. Here are a few questions to ask yourself:

- Does my decor suit the vibe that I'm trying to convey? Keep to your own personal aesthetic when choosing decor: your station, suite, or salon should speak of who you are in a fun way.

- Does the salon need any repairs? If yes, then get to it. Clients and staff notice these things. Do you have equipment that needs to be fixed? Faulty equipment is dangerous and should not be used until it's repaired or replaced.

- Am I utilizing my space the best I can? Try not to fill up the space so much that it looks cluttered. Make sure there is plenty of room for guests to walk around with ease.

- Is the salon as clean as it should be? Cleaning is a top priority. If the salon is not spotless, all your carefully-chosen decor means nothing. Keep it clean!

These questions are important because we all want a clean, safe, comfortable work environment that we are proud of. As you answer them, think about everything from your entryway and overall decorating style to the salon's paint colors, flooring, lighting, and more.

THE SALON ENTRANCE

The doorway and entrance to your salon should be inviting and draw people in. A clean entryway with a welcoming doormat will show that you care about your salon and its appearance. Make sure the outside is well lit, has a sign telling potential clients who you are and what you do, and is decorated to suit your style. The doorway is a great place to seasonally decorate. Changing your decor up for each holiday or with each change of season is fun and can create a really cool vibe that will pull clients in.

THE SALON DECOR

What is your salon style? Modern, contemporary, eclectic, retro, casual, artsy, industrial? Whatever your style, try to stick with the same decorating vibe throughout, as this will give a beautiful flow and cohesiveness to your space. We stylists tend to be very artistic, so use that ability to your advantage and get creative with your decor. Maybe you are an artist who likes to draw, paint, or create stained glass. Incorporating those talents into your decor would be a nice touch and would give your space some artistic flair. Do you scrapbook? If so, why not take pictures of your clients' hair and put the pictures into a scrapbook for all to see? If you enjoy sewing, you could make pillows, valances, or curtains to complement your space. Doing so will add interest to your decor, and clients will love to hear the stories behind these items.

Tastefully decorating your salon space will win clients over, because let's face it—they do sit for quite some time, so we may as well give them a nice space to be in. Try changing your artwork on a fairly regular basis, which is a fun way to change your decor without much work. Unsure about where to go for inspiration? You could check out home decor blogs and websites, browse through furniture stores, look through magazines and books, or head to a museum or art gallery. One of my favorite places to go for inspiration is consignment shops, which are filled with unique, gently used pieces of furniture and accessories at great prices.

If decorating does not come easily to you, then you may want to hire an interior decorator. The cost may be outweighed by the fact that you will have a beautiful space done just right to suit your taste. When you are deciding on the interior designer you would like to work with, make sure they have previous salon decorating experience, and have them show you their work. Being able to see what they are capable of will help guide you in making your decision. While working with a designer, you both should have a clear idea of what your vision is, so that they can bring your ideas to life and make them a reality.

CHOOSING YOUR WALL COLOR

The coloring you choose for the walls will have quite an impact on how you decorate, and may have the biggest impact out of any decorating decision on your guests. For instance, earthy tones can have a very soothing and relaxed feel, brighter colors can be bold and fun, and glitter can make a room feel exquisite. You can also paint one wall a vibrant, bright color to really make that wall pop. Keep in mind that you can always re-paint if you don't like how it looks. Be brave and go for a color that you're not sure about—it may be just the finishing touch you've been looking for.

FLOORING

Flooring can really add beauty to your space. First, you want to make sure that the flooring you choose is functional, durable, and easy to clean. Speak with a flooring expert about what it will take to properly maintain your floor. Tile, hardwood, or laminate are all very good choices. With any flooring you want to wipe up any spills as quickly as you can, so you won't have to deal with damage later on. Make sure to wash your floors on a regular basis. This will make a huge difference in the overall look and feel of your salon. If you are planning on putting a rug down, just make sure you can clean it easily. Try to keep your guests in mind when you're figuring out flooring. You don't want a client to trip over a rug that is too thick, or to have a rug slip out from under them because it has no padding underneath. Always keep the safety of all your guests in mind.

LIGHTING

Whatever your decorating style and colors, your space should always be light and bright. Natural lighting is best, so hopefully you have a few windows to let that light in. For your window treatments, try to stay away from anything that covers the windows too much. Blinds work well with a nice valance, which come in a variety of colors and patterns to suit any decor, or a sheer curtain. If you choose heavier curtains, make sure you can easily open them or use tie backs. Each of these options will offer privacy but also allow you to let in the light.

Don't fret if you are windowless; there are so many lighting options. Track lighting is nice due to the fact that you can adjust the angles (just be careful of shadows), and recessed lighting or even table and floor lamps are great options as well. Another idea is to have a few lights on a dimmer switch. In the right area, that will have a serene, tranquil effect.

DECORATING FOR ALL SEASONS

Seasonal and holiday decorating can also have a really nice effect on the salon. This is a great way to show your clients and stylists that you're putting effort into making their salon experience fun. Try to keep the style of your space in mind when decorating, keeping it simple and tasteful.

Highlighting certain areas of your salon while holiday decorating can be quite beneficial. For instance, Christmas is a great time for product sales, so why not put some extra decorating touches on your shelves? You can showcase your products in lovely gift bags or baskets, and hang lights around your display to really get some attention. Does your salon offer gift cards? Put them in small bags or boxes with tissue paper. Doing these things will help draw attention to what you are selling, and your clients will really take notice. Halloween is a fun holiday for decorating with lots of fun statues, lighting, and signs in vibrant purple, black, and orange colors. Think romance for Valentine's Day decor: your salon will look amazing with lots of hearts, cupids, and streamers in red, pink, and white. Or try white lights around a beautiful table set up with products in heart-decorated gift bags. Last but not least, don't forget decorating seasonally for winter, spring, summer, and fall.

KEEPING IT CLEAN

Cleaning is one of the most important ways to keep up with how the salon looks, and it needs to be done daily. Whoever is working on a particular day needs to help with the cleanup, unless you have hired someone to do this (*lucky!*). Pay close attention to the fine details when you clean, taking the time to sweep, vacuum, wipe windowsills, and regularly clean your products and shelves, counters, sinks, and mirrors. Sit down in your chair and look around from the client's perspective—you may be surprised to see fingerprints on the mirror or cobwebs in view. If you have plants, make sure they are watered regularly, the leaves are misted, and the dead leaves are taken off. Plants are beautiful in a salon, as long as they are taken care of. Keep your station clutter-free so you can use the space for products you are using on your guests. Your clients will really take notice of all these efforts, and will keep coming back.

Finally, there is one thing that has stood out to me over the years that I'd like to share: *Never* let a client sit down in your stylist chair before you have had a chance to clean. Always take a minute to wipe off the chair and sweep thoroughly. No one wants to sit in a chair that has another person's hair on it. I have seen stylists not clean up after their last guest, and I've also seen the look on the next client's face as they try to sit and look around at the mess. If I were that client, I might have run for the door. Our clients deserve better than this, so always be conscious of your cleanliness.

SCENT

You will service a variety of guests every day, and some, but not all of them, will get chemical services done. Some clients can be quite sensitive to these smells, so in this section I will talk about how to make the salon a bit more "scent friendly." With all the perms, colors, highlights, relaxers, and nail services being offered, the salon can get a bit, well, smelly! The products you use each come with their own unique scents, and typically there is not much you can do about that. However, there are some ways to make the salon environment a bit more pleasant for all.

GET THE AIR MOVING

Opening a window and letting in some fresh air is ideal —where possible and when the weather permits, this is really one of the best ways to let in fresh air and keep it circulating. Using a ventilation system is also a great way to vent out stale air and keep the air moving in the salon. Make sure the system is running properly, the filters are changed regularly, and that you have it professionally serviced. You can also use an air purifier. These are portable units that use fans to suck in the air through their filters, then push the cleaner air out. They remove odor, dust, and pollen from the air. They come in various sizes, so no matter the size of your salon, you should be able to find one that suits your needs. Look over the online reviews to get an idea of how loud the units are, how well they work, and how often you'll need to clean or change the filters.

CLEAN AND REFRESH

The best way to keep a fresh scent is to clean the salon daily with a spray cleaner or disinfecting wipes. Make sure to get the chairs and their bases, the sinks, and the work stations. Floors should be swept and vacuumed daily, and floor washing should be done once a week or biweekly. Take out the trash every day. Keep all of your soiled towels in a closed hamper with a lid. This will keep odors from getting out into the salon.

There are also a lot of scented products that you can use to make the salon fresh and clean smelling. I have a very light lilac room/linen spray that I use to create a relaxed feel. The first thing I do when I get into the salon is to give a light spray around the room, making sure to spray the linens, chairs, and towel bins. Another nice way to keep a scent lingering is to use a candle or an aromatherapy diffuser. What fragrance you use will depend on the effect you're trying to achieve. You can also make use of a seasonal fragrance, which is a nice way to get clients in the holiday spirit. Just be aware that you may have clients who are sensitive and/or allergic to candles and sprays. If you have guests with these types of sensitivities, make sure to write that down in your client binder so that you and others in the salon can refrain from using the scented products on the day of their appointment.

SOUND

The next time you enter your salon, listen. What do you hear? Talking, loud music, laughter, gossiping (oops)? What you are hearing sets the tone for your guests. Whatever you have envisioned your salon's vibe to be, the sound of your space will most definitely have a huge impact on what type of ambiance you are creating. For instance, a spa would benefit from peace, tranquility, soothing music, and soft voices to convey a feeling of relaxation, while an edgier salon may have louder rock music and be more boisterous. The sounds you choose will vary greatly depending on your salon's theme and vibe. In this section I will go over some ways to make your salon "listening friendly" for your guests.

MUSIC

The music in your salon should fit the style of your clients and stylists and your salon's overall vibe. Choose your music based on the feeling that you want your salon to convey. There are many genres of music that may provide the right fit, from classical to country to rock, soft rock, or top hits. Choose from the many radio stations available, or go online to really customize your playlist. Perhaps your salon would do well with a nice mix of music, or it may need to set a more specified tone. Whatever type of music you are playing, always try to keep the music at a volume that allows you to talk easily with your guest.

No matter the size of your salon, it is very important to stay professional at all times. Try to speak at a volume that your clients can hear, but not the entire salon. If you need to speak with someone, go directly over to them; don't shout from across the room. This is very unprofessional and could make clients feel uncomfortable.

AVOID GOSSIPING

Never speak badly of a coworker or client! Of course, in general you shouldn't speak badly of people at all, but it is especially important to avoid speaking badly of anyone to a client. The client in your chair may think, "Is this how she talks about me when I leave?" Or your client may actually know the person that you are trashing—how terrible would that be? Plus, you don't know who else may be overhearing the conversation that you're having in the salon. It's better to keep things positive, since you really don't want your salon to have a reputation for gossiping, and quality clients will not want to deal with all that drama.

Clients will get a feel for the salon by listening to the chatter amongst the stylists. If it is kept upbeat and everyone works together nicely, you will have happy clients. However, if there is bickering and general unpleasantness between stylists, clients will feel the tension, and it may push some clients out the door. No matter what, always take the high road and don't show any bitterness toward any others at work. The salon floor is definitely not the time or place to have it out.

QUESTION

When you have had services done elsewhere, what were the things that you liked about their atmosphere? Think about the three S's: sight, scent, and sound. On this list, is there anything you would find useful to implement at your salon?

_____

_____

_____

_____

_____

_____

_____

_____

TIME TO REFLECT AND
TAKE THE CHALLENGE

In this chapter you learned why sight, scent, and sound are important in keeping guests and stylists happy. Choose from one of the following two challenges:

(A) During a typical day in the salon, sit down at your station and observe everything you can.

How does the salon look? How does it smell? What does it sound like? Write down everything you can, including the pros and the cons. Then take all of your notes and think about how you can improve each of the cons. Next, look at the pros, and consider how can you make the most of this list and keep doing the things that are already having a positive effect.

(B) Go and have a service done at another comparable salon. Sit back, observe, and take it all in. You will get to see what it is like to be a guest and will gain a better understanding of what other guests may like or dislike about the overall experience. Follow the same steps listed in challenge A above to record your thoughts.

_____

_____

_____

_____

_____

_____

_____

_____

_____

_____

COMPETITION: IT'S ON!

———

We all have to face competition in our personal and professional lives, and being in the hair industry is no different. This industry can be very competitive, considering there is a salon on just about every corner. However, you have the power to turn this into a positive, rather than allowing it to hurt you or make you feel inadequate. When people are competing they tend to up their game, do their very best, and strive to win, so competition can motivate you in a very positive way. And there are a number of ways your competitors can even help you without ever knowing.

LEARN FROM THE COMPETITION

First of all, it is totally fine to check out the competition. Do a little friendly checking on some local hair salons by looking at their social media pages, websites, and online search listings. You will learn so much from browsing their sites, including:

- The types of services they offer and their pricing. As a stylist, you need to be aware of the pricing at local comparable salons in order to keep your prices competitive.
- The quality and style of their work. Looking at their client photographs can offer inspiration for color ideas, new and interesting haircuts, and perhaps unique ways of styling hair.
- How they photograph their guests. Do they use a really cool backdrop? Do they use a ring light or natural lighting? How do they pose their guests? Do they add a salon logo to their pictures?
- How they utilize social media to promote their business. How often are they posting on their social media pages? What type of content do they post?
- Their salon decor. Perhaps you have been considering doing some redecorating in your salon. Looking at how other salons have been decorated may give you some insight into design ideas, and possibly

provide the push you need to make your salon the absolute best it can be. Seeing how others have decorated will really make you want to up your game, which will resonate positively with your clients and stylists alike.

LOOK AT SALON REVIEWS

Reading online reviews may offer up some tips about what clients have liked or disliked about your competition. Pay attention to the wording in the reviews. For instance, how did the guest feel while in the salon? Did they enjoy a certain service? What was their overall feeling about the experience—were they happy and relaxed, or did they feel it was unpleasant and rushed? While reading the reviews, keep in mind that each person will have a vastly different experience while having the same service performed. For that reason, you should take online reviews with a grain of salt, using them only as a guide to help you get a feel for what has worked, or not, at other salons.

GO HAVE A SERVICE DONE

Perhaps it's time to check out your competition first-hand. Go and have a service performed at another salon or spa, perhaps a blowout, a deep conditioning treatment, or a trim. If you don't feel comfortable having a hair service performed, then perhaps try a massage, facial, makeup application, manicure, or eyebrow waxing. The lessons that can be learned here are invaluable.

A few things to observe:

- How did the salon present itself? Did it seem welcoming? When you entered, did it draw you in or make you want to run for the hills? Was the inside pleasant and clean? Was there a nice vibe to the space?
- How were you greeted when you walked in? Did the salon have a receptionist, or did a service provider come over to you? Did you feel welcome, or did they seem annoyed and put out?
- How was your service? Did the stylist or service provider ask you questions and make you feel comfortable? Did they take their time with you and make you feel like you mattered?
- How was payment handled? Did you feel the service was worth the cost?

While you are being serviced, be observant and take in as much information as you can, focusing on what you liked or disliked about the experience. Look around at the other service providers and their guests as well. Make some mental notes on the little things that they are doing to make sure their guests are having a great experience.

KINDNESS, COMPETITION, AND COWORKERS

Even a coworker can be classified as (good) competition. In your own salon, do you work with a stylist who dresses well, is professional and kind, and seems to ooze confidence? Does that stylist have a nice-sized clientele and treat them all with respect? If so, he or she would be a great role model to learn from. Why not ask this stylist questions about their work ethic, how they would handle certain situations, how they grew their clientele, or how they have marketed themselves successfully. In addition to being a great learning opportunity, it would be a nice compliment for your coworker to hear that you value their opinion. When we build each other up, we strengthen our salon community, which makes for a better work environment. Working together helps to maintain a friendly, upbeat, and strong salon.

OBSERVE YOUR COWORKERS

While working in your salon, you can learn so much from watching other stylists as they go through their days. Try doing a little casual observation, without staring or making it too obvious, since you don't want to make anyone feel uncomfortable. Don't think of this as competition; rather, consider it a way to be always watching, learning, growing, and upping your game. There are so many tips to learn from quietly watching others work and noticing how they interact with clients, apply color, handle consultations, or style certain types of hair. While observing, you may also see the things that you don't want to do with your guests. Hey, nobody is perfect! Anything that makes you cringe, or makes you think, "I would never want to be treated that way," is a great example of what not to do in your own work!

QUESTION

Do you feel negatively about, or intimidated by, competition? If so, reread this chapter and write down the positives that other stylists can teach you.

_____

_____

_____

_____

_____

TIME TO REFLECT AND
TAKE THE CHALLENGE

In this chapter you learned that competition isn't always a bad thing, and there is much to be learned from others. Make a list of salons or spas that you would like to go to for a service. Go online and check out their social media pages, reviews, and websites. Now pick a salon or spa from that list and go have a service done. While there, make some mental notes, relax, and enjoy yourself.

_____

_____

_____

_____

_____

_____

CHAPTER 6

THE NOT-SO-LITTLE THINGS

———

We have all heard the quote "it's the little things that mean a lot." When it comes to your clients, it is the little things you do for them that will endear you to them and keep them coming back. Obviously, doing a fabulous job on their hair consistently is key. But the list below includes all the other things that you can do to go above and beyond and to make your client feel extra special.

1. Offer your guest some refreshments. Some nice choices include coffee, tea, water, juices, and iced tea. A new seasonal hot or cold beverage would be a welcome change. You can also offer something to nibble on, such as crackers, homemade cookies, donuts, fruit, chocolates,

or muffins. If you have a client that is scheduled for a really long appointment, perhaps have cheese and crackers available, or you could even order a light lunch. Seasonal and holiday goodies are a nice touch. Try offering candies, cupcakes, or cookies in the spirit of the holiday. Having mints on your reception desk or at your stylist station is another nice treat. I have clients that always eat the mints I put out and make a huge deal over them.

2. When you have a client scheduled for a longer appointment, before you begin, ask if they need to use the restroom. This is a very simple gesture that shows your guest that you care about their comfort.

3. While shampooing your guest, ask them how the water temperature is feeling. Some clients like a very warm rinse, while others may prefer the water a bit on the cooler side. Their preference may vary, too, depending on the temperature outdoors, so for their comfort, always ask.

4. Invest in a padded neck rest for your sink. This will allow your guests to lean their heads back more comfortably and at the perfect angle.

They are easy to use and can be wiped dry, and are a must for any sink.

5. Have a lint brush on hand to remove those itchy, pesky cut hairs from your clients' clothing. This is a must since so many of our clients won't be going home to change after their salon visits.

6. Use powder with a soft brush or towel on your client's neck. This removes hair, and the powder will give a fresh, clean feel.

7. On occasion, give your client a free product sample. Try to choose a product that you think is a good fit. Write down in your client portfolio what you gave them, and always ask how they liked the product at their next appointment. Make sure you have that product for sale in the salon, just in case they want to purchase one the next time they come in.

8. Refer your clients to other professionals outside of your salon for services you don't offer. Have a list of really wonderful manicurists, massage therapists, waxing specialists, estheticians, or makeup artists available. By offering

up some names you are not only helping your guests, you are also helping out and building a relationship with another person in your industry. This can be a win-win when they send new guests your way.

9. Find something that will make you stand out as a stylist and give your clients a beautiful experience. Perhaps you do a relaxing scalp massage treatment, amazing blowouts, or killer braids. In your spare time you can reflect on your brand and come up with something that's all you. Read all you can on the subject, take classes, and make this your specialty. Whatever you come up with, don't keep it to yourself—make sure to blast it on social media, in the salon, and on your website to make sure your clients and future clients know what you're capable of doing. We all possess special, possibly hidden, talents. Now is the time to make yours known to the world!

10. Make sure you have current magazines and hair books for your guests to browse through, since most guests will have do some sitting when they come in for their appointment. Having wi-fi is also a really nice feature, especially if

you have clients who show up early, are scheduled for a longer service, or have to wait to be picked up after their appointment.

11. If your salon has a manicurist and they have some down time or have had a cancellation, ask them to come over to your guest and offer a mini-manicure or a hand massage free of charge. This is a wonderful treat for the guest, and the manicurist may get a new client for doing a great job and showing kindness. If your salon has a massage therapist, they could also do a relaxing hand, foot, or arm massage on your guest, again free of charge. Make sure when the mini-service is done, the client receives a business card or price list and perhaps a percentage off their first service.

12. Send a follow-up text or email asking the client how they like their new haircut, color, or style. Be enthusiastic with your wording. Ask questions about the new color or how it's been going styling the new haircut. Answer any questions they might have or suggest a product for their needs. Basically, you want the client to know that you are thinking of them and are willing to answer any questions they may have.

13. Confirm your clients' upcoming appointments with you. Get in the habit of calling, texting, or sending an email reminder before each appointment. Your clients will appreciate the time you took and the thoughtful reminder, and this will also help prevent missed appointments.

14. If possible, offer online booking. In this fast-paced world, it's nice for our clients to have the option to go online anytime and book with you. Online booking services allow clients to book an appointment with you and then receive automatic reminders.

15. Be welcoming and friendly. Your personality is unique and one of a kind. Your clients will naturally gravitate to you for a lot of reasons, but there are a few things that you can do to keep them coming back. Keep things upbeat, even when you're having issues at home or just feel "blah." Treat all of your guests with dignity and respect. These simple efforts will make each client's experience with you the very best it can be.

16. While styling your guest, tell them what you are doing to their hair and why. Hold the product in front of them and explain what it will

do for them. Clients love it when we tell them how to fix a problem. For instance, using a mousse or volume spray on fine, limp hair will create texture and fullness. To get a sleek look on curly or frizzy hair, show them how to use a smoothing cream or serum. Take your time and thoroughly explain why a particular product is right for them and what it does. There have been times when I put the product in their hands and explain to them how to apply the product correctly. When your guests are shown the proper way of applying the product, they can easily duplicate it at home. This is a very hands-on approach, and it is a great way to show them the amount to use and the correct placement.

17. Try to service only one guest at a time. I do this for every guest, but on occasion, I will add on a client if I know there will be a lengthy processing time. When you service one client at a time, it is not only good for your client, it's also good for you. The idea here is that you will have a breather (including time to eat, drink, and rest) between clients and will not feel so overwhelmed, and your guest won't feel rushed around or neglected. Try this out sometime,

and I think you will find that most clients appreciate the time you spend with just them.

18. Take your time with your guests. Have you ever had a service done and felt like the service provider was rushing through the process? That is really not a good feeling, and it may have discouraged you from returning. Now think about your clients. They will not get a good feeling if they are rushed from start to finish. Clients will know that they are being hurried along, and while they may not say anything, they also may not come back. Don't risk that happening. Taking your time on your clients will show them that you care, which will be totally appreciated.

19. Become intuitive with your guests. When you're getting to know a client, listen to them and really take in what they are saying so you can get to know their personality. Then it will become very easy for you to pick up on their cues. Maybe they had a rough day and aren't in a talking mood—this is good for you to know, so you can adjust the level of conversation. Or they may be feeling a little blah, in which case you can be extra positive in hopes of cheering

them up. Being able to "read" your guests is a gift and should be used to make every experience with every guest the best it can be.

20. Once the initial consultation is done, let your clients talk without interruption. Clients really just want to be heard. Their time in your chair is their chance to talk about themselves, and what they really want is for you to listen. You want them to trust you and feel comfortable enough to have these conversations with you. So to keep this openness going, try not to pass judgement, give advice only when asked, and be present in the conversation.

QUESTION

When you have a service done, what are the little things that make you happy and keep you going back?

_____

_____

_____

_____

_____

_____

TIME TO REFLECT AND
TAKE THE CHALLENGE

In this chapter you learned why it's the little things that mean the most. Reread this chapter. Take two of the ideas that really resonate with you and implement them at your salon. You may be surprised at how making little changes can mean so much to your guests.

_____

_____

_____

_____

_____

_____

_____

CHAPTER 7

PICTURE PERFECT

———

The chance to be featured as a model on your social media platforms can be very exciting for your clients. Asking to photograph them will show them that they have what it takes to be in the spotlight on your pages, and will give them a boost of confidence and make them feel quite special. Most clients will love having their picture taken and enjoy seeing it come up on your social media pages, but there are some camera-shy guests that won't want any part of it. Always get your client's permission, ideally in writing, before posting any photos of them.

Sharing photos of your work is an opportunity to show the world what you do and how good you are at doing it. Below are some tips to help you get the most out of photographing your clients and using those photos to help build your brand.

THE IMPORTANCE OF LIGHTING

While taking your client's picture, always keep lighting in mind. This is probably the most important aspect of getting a perfect picture. Natural light is best, so if you can find a nice spot just outside of your salon that has a little filtered sun, that would be ideal. Try to avoid direct sunlight, as it can cast some unflattering shadows. If you don't have the ability to trek outside, try to find an area of the salon that is nearest to a window, door, or a skylight—anything that lets in some natural light.

Another great option is to use a ring light. This is a circular light that shines a very specific light on your subject, and you take a picture through the middle. There are many benefits to using a ring light: it gives off an even light, reduces harsh shadows, gently balances skin tone, and enhances the color of the hair. And the best part is, you don't have to leave the salon space to get really well-lit pictures. Just set up the light anywhere and click away.

The background for the pictures should be kept clean and simple. It's hard to focus on your subject if you have lots of clutter in the background. Instead go for something subdued, like a lovely brick wall, beautiful tree, flowering bush, painting, plain backdrop, or staircase. A nice way to subtly keep your guest in the spotlight is to fade out the background. This will make the client "pop" in the picture.

PHOTOGRAPH WHAT YOU DO BEST

When you choose a client to photograph, do something unique with their hair that will make you stand out as a stylist; something exceptional that will pull potential clients to you. We have all been there, scrolling through our feeds when we come to a photo that brings us to a complete halt! That's the idea, to get all your potential clients to stop, look, and then check out your hair page. Maybe your extraordinary talent is braiding, updos, fashion color, baylayage, precision cutting, or eyebrow shaping. Whatever your specialty is, showcase your talent and let your future clients know what you're all about through your photos.

When you take the pictures, make sure you are happy with every aspect of how the client's hair looks. Look for flyaway hair, especially if you're photographing outside and it's breezy. Take pictures from every angle, including the front, back, and sides, and make sure to take quite a few pictures so you will have many to choose from.

Try taking some detail photos as well, and really pinpoint a specific focal point. Focus on a beautiful hair accessory, the swoop of a bang, a single curl, or an elegant braid. A photograph like this can be very striking and beautiful. Taking before-and-after pictures can also make a huge impact, especially if it's a dramatic change, and potential clients will enjoy seeing what you are capable of from start to finish. Take pictures through the process of a new cut, color, or updo, or have a coworker take pictures of you while you are working. This adds visual interest to your posts, and will give your future clients a glimpse of you doing what you love.

INVEST IN A DIGITAL CAMERA

Depending on how much you are willing to spend on photographing your clients, you may want to invest in a digital camera. There are many benefits to using a good digital camera, including better quality when uploading your images, easier-to-control lighting, more editing options, truer color, and complete focus on your guest using telephoto lenses. Obviously there is an expense to buying a digital camera, but prices do vary. Go online and research different cameras to find the one that is best for you and fits your budget. Having a nice camera may be exactly what you need to get the absolute best photographs possible.

CELL-PHONE PHOTOGRAPHY

Cell phones are a simple, manageable choice that most people are very familiar with and never leave home without. Most of us already have an extensive knowledge of exactly how to use our phones to take pictures, which makes this option effortless. Most phones have built-in features that can be used to enhance our photographs, including filters and cropping, editing, sharpening, brightness, and contrast tools. These features are terrific when used with a light touch. What you don't want to do is alter the photo so much that it doesn't even look like your client anymore. Really put the work into doing a lovely job on your guest, and you be able to achieve a more real photograph without the need to over-edit.

POSTING YOUR PHOTOS

When you are ready to post the pictures, make sure to really check them over first. Look at the background— does it have a clean look? Is there clutter? Check the mirrors carefully. Is there clutter in the reflection? Do you see people standing around? These are the little details that should not be overlooked when deciding what you want to post.

When you think you are ready, here are a few ideas to help you post on your social media pages:

1. Choose a time that will get plenty of views. You can do an online search to find out the best times to post on each platform, then

make sure you are posting at peak times to increase your traffic.

2. If you have a salon page (and you should), post the pictures to that page first, then share to your personal page. This is a good way to get more of your friends to see the content of your salon page and then like your page. The more friends you have to like, comment on, and share your content, the greater reach it will have.

3. Tag the client in the photo. Again, this will help get more eyes on the post.

4. Post before-and-after pictures together to make a bigger impact.

5. Search through hashtags to find the best ones for your pictures and use them to help get you noticed.

6. Encourage your friends, family, and clients to comment on and share your posts. This will help your photos to reach lots of potential clients.

7. Come up with your very own theme, such as adding your logo on the photo, doing a collage, or using a special frame or border. Your theme should be something that you do to your pictures that is all you. Make it a focal point on every photograph you post, and it will set you apart and make people remember you.

8. Whatever you consistently put out on social media is what you will attract. You may be completely fine with a very specialized social media presence, but if you want to attract a more diverse clientele, you'll need to mix things up and not always post the same things. It's good for future clients to see that you have a wide range of abilities. For example, if you have a mixed-age clientele, but are only posting photos of younger clients, perhaps it's time to start including your more mature guests in your portfolio. You may be surprised to learn how many mature clients are active on social media, so include them!

TAKING PICTURES OF YOUR SALON

Now that you've perfected the art of photographing your clients, why not take the time to snap some pictures of your salon space? Whether you rent a booth or a suite or are a salon owner, getting beautiful pictures of your space can really be an asset and a way to draw in potential clients.

The photos you take can be used for your website and social media pages, and can be highlighted in your online search presence. I use one of my salon pictures on my referral cards to give any new clients a glimpse of what my salon looks like before they enter the door.

Your potential clients will appreciate getting a preview of what the salon looks like before their first visit or before they call to schedule an appointment.

Staging your salon is an important step before you start clicking away. The first thing you want to do is to clean, clean, clean! Remove clutter, only have out a couple of bottles of shampoo and conditioner at the sink, make sure your product shelves are organized and clean, open up the curtains or blinds to make the salon light and bright, and make sure any artwork and rugs are straightened up. Focus on the space only, with no people in the shot, and check the mirror reflections to make sure you're not visible. Really put in the effort and the results will make you very proud, and potentially draw in new guests.

PROMOTING YOURSELF
THROUGH PHOTOS

Your clients and your salon space are both vital parts of your business to photograph—and so are you! Now may be a good time to think about having pictures taken of you in the salon or while working on a client. You can have a coworker take the pictures, or you could go with a professional photographer. Either way, having well-thought-out pictures to use on your website, social media, or salon menu and referral cards will show the world how happy you are doing what you love.

Here are a few tips to keep in mind when taking pictures of yourself in the salon:

- You will command more attention if you dress professionally. This will make you look like the leader you are.
- Your hair should look its best, since this is a big part of what you are promoting.
- Add a bit more makeup than you usually wear. When being photographed you may look a bit washed out, depending on the lighting. If you typically don't wear makeup, think about using a colored lip gloss or maybe some blush to add a little color.
- Have fun with different poses. Stand behind your stylist chair or desk, sit in your chair, and stand in the entrance or in the middle of the salon. Work it!
- Have a group photo taken of all the salon workers. This is a nice way for new clients to see who works in the salon, and the photo can be used on your salon website and social media pages.

Here are a few tips for having yourself photo-graphed while working on a client:

- Again, dress nicely and make sure your hair and makeup are done well for this photo shoot. Wear clothes that express your personality.
- Choose a client or friend to work on who will enjoy being photographed and will enhance the photos.
- Have fun and experiment with different poses. Try having the photographer change their position around to get multiple perspectives of you and what you're doing.
- Keep talking and smiling while you're being photographed. Perhaps telling a funny story will make everyone feel comfortable. Having your photo taken may feel a bit weird at first, but just be you, have fun, and go with it. The idea here is for the pictures to capture the true vibe of your salon.

QUESTION

How can you add your own "brand" to the pictures that you will be posting to make them really stand out?

_____

_____

_____

_____

_____

TIME TO REFLECT AND TAKE THE CHALLENGE

In this chapter you learned the importance of photographing your guests, your salon, and yourself. In the space below, come up with a list of clients to photograph, clients to have yourself photographed with, and potential photographers. Then write a list of all the potential social media sites, websites, and online review sites you can post your pictures on. Once you have compiled your lists, start taking action and get some really great pictures out into the world.

_____

_____

_____

_____

_____

CHAPTER 8

THE NEW STYLIST

———

If you are a new stylist, congratulations! When you are just starting out in the industry, everything is fresh, new, and very exciting. In the beginning, you should take some time to figure out where and how you would like to start your career. Do you want to get right to it, by applying for a stylist position, or would you like to ease into the business with some help? Are you thinking of starting at a chain salon, a local salon, or a day spa? Luckily in this business you will have some options when it comes to your next step.

FIND A MENTOR

If you're planning to get right to work in a salon, you may want to focus on finding one that will help you gain experience through a mentor. A mentor is someone already working in the industry who has built up a clientele and would like to coach you on the ins and outs of being a stylist. Your mentor will be your go-to person if you need help with anything salon-related. They are also a person you will watch and learn from and spend quite a bit of time with, so make sure your mentor is professional, patient, and helps you when you need it, and that the two of you click. Being mentored can be extremely valuable in guiding you through the process of becoming a proficient stylist, with your mentor there for you whenever you need help.

BECOME AN ASSISTANT

Another idea is to become a salon assistant. This works very well for stylists who are still in school, as the salon may hire you after you have been licensed, or for those who are just getting into the business and yet still want a very hands-on approach to easing into salon life. As an assistant, you will do whatever is asked of you to help the team of stylists, such as greeting guests and offering them a beverage, answering the phone, stocking retail shelves, shampooing, sweeping, and keeping the salon neat. In this role you can learn so much about the business by assisting many different senior stylists. You will learn varying techniques from stylists who have made a name in our industry and are willing to let you assist in their day-to-day salon activity. When you assist, you will have a great opportunity to observe a range of cutting techniques, unique color application styles, finishing or styling methods, and ways of interacting with guests on the phone, in the front of the salon, and while they are being serviced. While you are assisting you will be learning a great deal, and this will help you figure out what works for you. During your tenure as an assistant you should remain professional, courteous, and upbeat, dress nicely, and always be willing to help. If you are still in cosmetology school and are considering becoming an assistant, it may be a good idea to call your State Board of Cosmetology to find out exactly what an assistant is able to do in your state.

START AT A SALON

You could also go right to work at a local salon or a larger corporate-type salon. The salon you choose should have a constant flow of new clients—or you could choose a strictly walk-in salon. Working at either of these types of salons, you won't have to worry about not being busy enough. Generally there will be a steady stream of clients due to the salon's location, convenient hours, and lower prices that get people in the door. The corporate-type salons can be a great place to start. They are generally busy and some of them may offer you benefits, such as paid vacation time, holiday pay, continuing education, and health insurance. These are all very important factors for you to consider when you start looking. The first several salons that I worked in had a steady stream of walk-in business (in fact, one was strictly walk-in), so I was kept very busy and quickly overcame any fear I may have had because I quickly gained experience. Either one of these salon situations would be a great way to learn, boost up your confidence, and start building up that all-important clientele.

One thing that I would suggest you *not* do as a new stylist is jump right into booth renting. Even if the salon you rented in had adequate walk-ins, it would not be enough to ensure that you would build up and retain your own client list. To be a booth renter, you will first need a decent-sized clientele comprised of people that have been with you for some time and have shown, at least to some degree, that they are committed to staying loyal to you. Before you can reach that point, you'll need to gain hands-on experience while learning from senior stylists. You would also need to have a good understanding of the business in regards to finances and buying and keeping track of your stock, product lines, equipment, and promotional materials. Being a booth renter is a wonderful career choice, but it is one that you may want to consider later on in your career, when you have gained a solid knowledge of salon life and have more experience.

VISIT POTENTIAL SALONS

When you become licensed you will want to go out and visit as many salons as you can. Write down any questions that you would like to ask. For instance, do you have a mentoring program? How do walk-in clients get divided? What are the incentives for product sales? What hours will I be working? If I have questions, who do I see? Is the pay hourly, with commission-based incentives? Do you have in-salon education or do you compensate for classes? You get the idea. Go online and research the websites and social media feeds of salons in your area to see if you would like to go and check them out. When you are going on these tours, always ask to speak with the salon owner or manager, since they are the ones that do the hiring. Don't worry about rejection— some of the salons you visit may not have any openings, but you can still leave a nice impression by thanking them for their time and leaving a resume. If you have never made up a resume, ask a friend, family member, or teacher at your school for help. Your resume should include any work experience, special classes you've taken, school information, and any other experience you have relating to hair, customer service, or finance.

WATCH AND LEARN

Once you have started working in a salon, try to be as observant as possible. Always watch and learn from the other stylists—the senior stylists are the ones to focus on, since they have years of experience. If you are being mentored or assisting, then you will already be observing. However, if you have decided to get right to it and start on the floor, then this advice is extremely important. Being new to the business can sometimes be hard. With that in mind, the more you can pay attention to the way the senior stylists do hair and interact with their guests, the easier this whole transition will be for you. Talking with stylists, observing what they are doing, and asking questions will give you insight into how the salon runs and how to go above and beyond for your guests. I have learned so much from the very talented stylists and salon owners I've had the pleasure of working with over the years, and the experience I gained from each of those salons has been invaluable. I'm glad I was able to experience working in a wide variety of salons, as they all aided me in my journey to find what was just right for me.

ATTRACT NEW CLIENTS

When you are new to the business, make sure to put yourself "out there" so future clients will know who you are, what you do, and where to find you. Here are a few tips on how to do that:

- Talk to everyone you know and make them aware of where you work and what you do. If you really enjoy or specialize in one particular area, let them know that too.

- Hand out cards to people you meet, and ask your friends and family to do the same.

- Mention where you are working on all of your social media pages. As you go along, take pictures of your clients and start posting. You can also post when you are working and when you have openings.

- If the salon that you are working in does not have much of a social media presence, perhaps you could talk to the owner or manager and get something set up for them. Not every salon owner is great with every social media platform, and taking the initiative to help is a nice thing for you to do that will show interest on your part and possibly get some new clients into the salon, which is good for everyone!

- Ask the salon manager if you could do a special offer to help get your name out there and get new people through the door. Some salons are willing to do this, but you won't know unless you ask!

MAKE YOURSELF INDISPENSIBLE

Whatever salon you decide to work in, make sure you go above and beyond what is being asked of you. This is the time to make a good impression and make a name for yourself in your salon. Here are a few ideas that will really make you stand out as a new stylist:

- Clean like your life depends on it. Then, when you think you're done cleaning, keep going!
- Ask other stylists if they need help with anything. This sets a nice tone with your coworkers, and they will love the fact that you are willing to help out.
- Show up early and stay for as long as they need you.
- If a stylist is running late, ask them if they need any help. Wouldn't you want to be helped out, if it were you?
- Don't gossip. Who needs that drama?
- Be friendly, polite, and approachable.
- Pay attention to your hair, makeup, and clothing, and make sure they all scream out "you." Remember, your vibe will attract your ideal clients to you.
- If you are needed on your day off, then go in. Be that person that goes above and beyond.

STICK WITH IT

I have been a stylist for many years, and my advice for you, the new stylist, is, don't give up! We have all been there, and it's not easy by any means. You will have ups and downs while you are still learning and getting used to being hands-on. Clients can be intimidating, and so can coworkers who have many years of experience. Just make sure you are in a salon where your colleagues will answer questions, be considerate of your needs, and help you grow, and that you surround yourself with people that are nice and helpful. So many new stylists call it quits early on, and maybe for some that's the right decision. But if you love doing hair and making clients look and feel their best, then stick with it. There are so many reasons to stay in the business:

1. You are able to be creative while doing something fun that you love.
2. You'll have the flexibility to work the hours you want, and down the road when you become a booth renter, suite renter, or salon owner, you will have the freedom to adjust your schedule to suit your needs perfectly, whether that means working part time, full time, or anything in between.

3. If you are consistent with your work, are kind and courteous, show up consistently, and generally care about people and their time, then you will be paid well.

4. You get to be a problem solver, helping to resolve problems both with clients' hair and in their lives.

5. You'll have the opportunity to work alongside some of the most vibrant, caring, and fun humans ever.

6. You will be able to attend fun classes and crazy-fun hair shows to further your education.

7. You will meet so many wonderful clients, and these relationships will truly enrich your life.

8. You get to make your clients feel good about themselves. This is one of the best things about being a stylist, because there is nothing quite like that feeling when a client looks in the mirror in total amazement at how they look, thanks to you!

Growing your clientele will not happen overnight. This will actually be one of the biggest challenges you will face in your career. In fact, it will take many years of consistency, branding, posting, talking to people you meet, handing out cards, and, as your career progresses, putting into place a really well-thought-out referral program. Doing these things will get you going in the right direction as a new stylist. The time and effort that you put in today will pave the way for a fulfilling career for your future.

STAND OUT AND BE NOTICED

There is a salon on just about every corner, so how do you get noticed when you are just starting out? Be authentically you—this is a must, and the right clients will gravitate to you for this reason. Stand out by being nice, kind, and helpful. Care about people and how you make them feel. Have fun while you are working on your clients—this will make it a pleasant experience for them and for you. Love your work, because when you do, it shows in everything you do, and that vibe will get you noticed. Be positive. Clients want to be with a stylist with an enthusiastic attitude, not someone who is negative (leave all that at the door). All of these things you do will make your guests happy, and make them want to refer their friends and family to you. This is how you start to build that stellar client base that is absolutely essential for your future.

QUESTION

Think about what kind of salon you would prefer to work at. Are you ready to get right into a salon, do you need a mentor, or would you like to assist first? What is your ideal working situation?

_____

_____

_____

_____

_____

_____

TIME TO REFLECT AND
TAKE THE CHALLENGE

In this chapter you, the new stylist, learned a few things about what it takes to be in this business. Go online and research the salons in your area. Make a list below of all the salons you would like to visit. Then visit each salon one by one, making sure to bring your resume.

_____

_____

_____

_____

_____

_____

CHAPTER 9

THE ART OF GIVING

One of the great things about our industry is our power to help others. You probably don't think too much about how you truly affect other people, but on a daily basis, you give confidence to others and make your guests feel really good about themselves. Once you open yourself up to the art of giving, you will see how rewarding being a stylist can truly be. By implementing some of the ideas in this chapter, you will not only be making someone truly happy, you will also be putting your good name out into the world.

WRITE A CARD

Have you received a card lately? If you have, you probably got pretty excited. The art of writing letters and cards is fading fast with the ubiquity of emails and texting. So how nice would it be for your clients to receive a card from you? You could either mail it or hand it to them at the end of their service. They will not be expecting it, but will absolutely love the gesture. In the card you could thank them for being such a wonderful, loyal client and give them a small token, such as a percentage off on their next service or a small free service like a deep conditioning treatment, a bang trim, or a mini scalp massage at the sink. They will appreciate any of these things and it will truly make their day.

GIVE A GIFT

On occasion, why not give a sample product or a small gift to a loyal client? The gift can be something small that happened to make you think of them, or a trial-sized product that your client has mentioned they would like to try or that you think will benefit their particular hair type. Whatever it is that you are giving them, present it wrapped in some way with a notecard telling them that you appreciate them and think of them often.

I had a longtime client who was turning sixty, so I decided to do something for this special occasion. Because I knew how much he enjoyed getting his hair washed and feeling pampered, I gave him a gift certificate for a scalp massage treatment, all wrapped up in a special gift bag, because presentation means a lot. His reaction was pure joy, and it turned out it was the first gift he had been given for this birthday.

Do you like to bake? Having homemade cookies, cakes, brownies, or breads in the salon would be an especially nice treat for your clients. Maybe your guests are coming to you straight from work, from running errands all day, or at dinner time. Having homemade goodies available will really go over well—plus, you want happy clients during your appointments, not hungry ones!

VOLUNTEER

Donate your time and skills at a local school for the theater department, music department, or a school fashion show. I volunteered for three years at a local high school, doing hair for their theater department. I was extremely proud to have been a part of creating the right looks for the students. I was able to give back to my community with my creativity, and I got exposure through my name being featured in the play's program, and through the pictures that were posted on social media. The best part for me, though, was working with these very talented students and being able to style their hair, which gave them more time to focus on their roles.

Another way to volunteer your time is to provide a gift certificate for your services to a church raffle or other organization that is doing a fundraiser. There are many organizations that are in need of donations. Choose a service to give such as a free cut, blowout, or eyebrow waxing. Whatever you offer will help a good cause, bring in a new guest, and put your name out into the world, where it should be.

I personally have given out numerous services to be raffled off at schools, churches, and hospitals. I've also been involved in several cut-a-thons, which is when a stylist or group of stylists does haircuts, usually at a discounted rate, and then gives all the proceeds to a person in need or a charity. I organized one cut-a-thon for a heart transplant recipient's GoFundMe account. I advertised it on social media and had an amazing turn-out—I even had people come into the salon that didn't need a haircut at the time, but just wanted to donate. The opportunity to give to someone through my own effort made this one of the best experiences I have had as a stylist.

HOLD A MAKEOVER FOR CHARITY

Another great way to raise money for charity is by organizing a makeover event. You could ask all the stylists at your salon if they would like to style hair and possibly do a little makeup for a good cause, then contact a local photographer, possibly one that is just getting started in the business and would like the recognition, to see if they would like to come to the salon to take the pictures. Anyone that is participating would get their hair styled, their makeup done, and a professional picture taken. They would pay a set fee, with all the proceeds going to whatever charity you'd like. To advertise the event, use social media, contact your local newspaper, and hand out flyers to your guests. This is a fun way to get the team together and help out those in need. Make sure to have a photo of all the stylists taken and post on your salon's social media pages and website.

HELP A LOCAL FOOD PANTRY

Local food pantries are always looking for donations. Set up a box in the salon in which your clients can drop off nonperishable food items. In return, you could put the names of the clients who have dropped off items into a raffle to win a gift bag or basket filled with hair products or accessories, or a free service. This is a nice way to help out the less fortunate and give your valued clients a gift for doing their part.

Around the holidays you can set up a large box for Toys for Tots. This is a great organization that distributes toys to the less fortunate. Let your clientele know about this ahead of time and make sure you are posting about it on social media. Another nice thing that you as a salon can do is to put up a family giving tree. Go to a local church or other charitable organization and ask for a gift list for a family in need. Once you get the list of what your particular family would like, hang paper ornaments on the tree, each with a different gift printed out on it. If a stylist or client would like to participate, they would pick an ornament from the tree and purchase that gift. Then you can either put the bought gifts under the tree or in a large box until it's time to deliver them.

REACH OUT TO THOSE IN NEED

I had a friend who was going through a very difficult time and I wanted to do something special for her. I got in touch with her and let her know that I would love to do a color and cut for her, free of charge. This was one small thing that I could do for her in the midst of all her chaos. She was able to come in for some "me time," and it gave her some much-needed relaxation. You probably have clients that have gone through some pretty tough situations. Why not offer those clients a nice service that will lift their spirits?

Perhaps you can offer to go to someone's home to do their hair after they've had surgery, or if they are unable to leave their home due to an injury. Or you can do an updo for a girl going to prom at a discounted rate or free of charge. Prom is a big deal, and everyone should have the opportunity to look their best and feel good about themselves. Similarly, if you know of a family in need around the holidays, offer to do their cuts for free—this will make them look good and you feel good. Whatever the reason, take advantage of the opportunity to step up, help out, and give. We all need to understand the great gifts that we possess, and the ability to help others who have hit hard times in their lives is one of those gifts. Doing good for others will make you feel terrific, and is so very worthwhile.

QUESTION

What ways can you come up with to give back
to your community?

_____

_____

_____

_____

_____

_____

_____

TIME TO REFLECT AND
TAKE THE CHALLENGE

In this chapter you learned about making a difference in someone's life through the art of giving. Write down a contribution you can make
that will help someone and give them (and you)
great joy. Make a detailed plan, then go do it.
You will be glad you did—and so will they!

_____

_____

_____

_____

_____

_____

_____

CHAPTER 10
KEEPING A DETAILED RECORD

Whether you have a client binder or notebook or are using a computer to log information about your guests, a clear record-keeping system is an important tool to help you focus on your clients and a great way to keep detailed information about them. A client's file should always include the basics, including their name, address, email address, and cell and home numbers (an absolute must, in case you need to cancel or change an appointment). If the client was referred to you, make a note of who did the referring so you can thank them later, and also record any other general information you may need.

Each client file should contain two separate sections: one strictly for their hair and the other about their life. The day of their appointment is the best time to review your notes. This will keep the information fresh in your mind. Look over your notes on all the clients that you will be servicing that day. Make sure to keep an eye out for anything you did differently at their last appointment; that way you can ask them how that particular change has been working out for them.

THE HAIR SECTION

This section will contain all of the pertinent information about your client's hair. Keep a record of their appointment dates, likes, and dislikes. Make sure to include any details you need to keep your clients comfortable. For instance, I have a guest who doesn't like me to use powder on his neck, so I wrote that down. Maybe you have a client with sensitive skin and you use a barrier cream around their hairline—make a note of that. Did your guest have an allergic reaction to a particular color or perm or styling product? If so, you would absolutely want that documented. Keep your notes updated with current prices, especially if there was an increase from the last time they were in. Keep a record of products used or anything they buy from you, so that at their next appointment you can ask how they liked the new gel, shampoo, deep conditioner, or hair spray and keep it in stock for them. For color treatments, write down which color you used, the timing, how much color was used (so you don't waste the product), and how you applied it. For a perm you should write down what was used (perm solution, rod size, and placement), and for how long it processed. Did you do a different haircut on your guest? Write it down. Are they styling it differently? If you used clippers, which guards did you use? Are they growing out their bangs? Did you do a dry cut? Were thinning shears or a razor used? Remembering all of these things is important to maintain a happy client. Wouldn't you hate to finish a haircut only to hear, "don't you remember, we changed my hair last time, I'm wearing it on the other side," or, as you are cutting away, to hear, "remember, I'm letting my bangs grow out"? You can't possibly remember every little detail, and when you document it you won't have to.

THE LIFE SECTION

For this section, write down anything having to do with your client's life. Where do they live? Where do they work? Include all of their telephone numbers: work, cell, and home. When not at work, what do they enjoy doing? Do they travel or play sports? What days and times are convenient for them to come in and see you?

If you have clients who are related, jot that down. Perhaps your client enjoys a particular beverage—make a note of that so you can have it on hand at their next appointment. When your clients talk about a particular restaurant, bar, concert venue, travel destination, or any other recommendation, write it down. This is great information for you to know, not only so you can go and try the recommendation out yourself, but also so you can pass the suggestion along to your other guests. Recommendations like these are invaluable, especially to a small local business, to help bring in new customers to these credible establishments. Because you'll service a lot of people on a weekly basis and it's impossible to remember every detail, keeping these notes will help you get to know your guests while keeping them happy.

I've found that the best time to write my notes is while my client is processing or right after they leave. This way their service is still very fresh in my mind, and I can write down all those small details before I forget. It may not always be possible to write at those times, and that's fine, just take a few minutes at the end of the day. Believe me, when they come in for their next appointment you'll be glad you took the time to write down all those special notes.

NEW IDEAS

The client binder is also a great place to write about new ideas that you may have for a particular guest. We have all been there: we pass someone in a store, see a picture online or in a magazine, or see someone on television and think, "my client would look great with that color or haircut." This is exactly the sort of thing you want to write about and remember. Clients love when you can give them fresh ideas for their hair.

OTHER USEFUL INFORMATION

Medical and other personal information can also be helpful to write down and remember. For example, take note of any ear piercings, especially in the upper cartilage, eyebrow piercings, moles or cysts on the scalp, scalp conditions such as sensitive skin, psoriasis, eczema, or alopecia, or scalp injuries, including stitches. Does your guest have special needs? Be sure to write down how you can accommodate your special-needs guest to make them as comfortable as you can. When a client has had surgery it is vital to know what they had done, their recovery time, and how you can make them comfortable for the time that they are with you. Are they able to lean back into a sink? Do they need a stool to rest their legs on? Are they able to walk around the salon, or do they need assistance? Knowing all of this information is important for the comfort and safety of your guest.

QUESTION

Can you come up with a few ideas of your own that you would like to keep track of in your client binder?

_____

_____

_____

_____

_____

_____

TIME TO REFLECT AND
TAKE THE CHALLENGE

In this chapter you learned why keeping detailed and thoughtful records about your guests is important. Start a client binder today. Go through your appointment schedule and write your clients' names and all the details that you can think of from their previous appointments. By their next appointment, you will be glad you did.

_____

_____

_____

_____

_____

_____

_____

FOCUSING ON THE ESSENTIALS

In this chapter you will learn about a variety of topics that are essential to the business, from the consultation process, to the importance of pre-booking clients and charging what you're worth, to losing clients and rectifying mistakes, and how staying positive will give your career a boost.

1. Have a consultation with every single client that sits in your chair, whether you have been doing their hair for six months or twenty years. This should be part of your service to them. Ask the questions that you need answered, listen to their responses, then give your professional opinion on what you believe will look best and how it can be achieved and maintained. Be confident and lead the consultation

by asking as many questions as you can to get a real clear picture of what your guest wants. This is where the stylist-client communication begins.

For a new guest, the consultation should be quite lengthy. This is the time to ask questions and get to know your new guest. The type of questions to ask would include: Tell me what you like or dislike about your hair? Would you like me to do some layering, or do you prefer one length? Would you like a face-framing bang? What is your level of commitment to coming back every four to six weeks for your trim or color? What tools and products do you use to style your hair at home? Do you prefer a wash-and-wear style? How much time are you willing to spend styling your hair? Let them answer and really listen to what they are saying. Have a good dialogue with your guest and offer your ideas, including a timeline of when they should return and what they can do at home to keep up their style. Only when the full consultation is over and you both understand what the day's service will entail, should you begin.

For your existing clients, you will still have a consultation, but with a different set of questions. Your consultation may sound something like this: How was your last visit? Was your new style easy for you to duplicate at home? How was your last color?

Did you like the new product we tried out last time? What you want to do is to mention anything new that you did at their last visit and ask if they liked the change. This is why writing down details about their appointments is necessary, so you can refresh your memory before their next appointment. Just as you would with a new guest, offer up some new ideas and product suggestions. It is so important to give them fresh ideas, which lets them know you have been thinking about them since their last appointment.

Remember that you should never mix up any color before your guest has arrived and has had their consultation, even for existing clients. There are two reasons for this: first, you may decide during the consultation to change the color formulation. Each time your guest comes in, you should fully expect to change up the formula (perhaps just a little), so having it already made up would be a waste. And second, your client may not show up! Even with a confirmation text or email, things happen and they may be a no-show for the day, which would again be a waste of color.

During any consultation, always give your guests expert advice on what cut will suit their particular facial shape and hair texture, how color will add dimension or accentuate their skin tone, and what they will need to do to maintain the look. Also, it is perfectly acceptable to decline a service to a client during the consultation. You will gain more respect by refusing to do a chemical service on a client with already-compromised hair, than by doing the service and completely destroying any integrity the hair may have had left. Instead, suggest putting the client on a special plan of deep conditioning or hair mask treatments, regular trims, and an at-home hair-care regimen. You are in charge of what you do, so if it doesn't feel right, don't do it!

2. Focus on the foundations of our business. Make sure you are doing really good cuts, whether with scissors, clippers, thinning shears, or a razor. Learn as many new styling techniques as you can. Know the basics of color—this is essential for understanding how certain undertones will affect the appearance of color. Make sure you know which cuts look best on different face and body shapes. Teach your clients what products they should be using at home and how they can achieve the desired look with those products.

3. Have as much product knowledge as you can, both about the products you are using in the salon, and those you have recommended for your guests' home care. To be able to give your guests the best products for their hair, you will need to understand

why they work, how much to use, and how to apply them properly. Only then can you teach your guests how to successfully use them at home.

4. Be a consistent stylist. Build your brand on the principle of consistency. Clients love the familiarity of returning to a consistent stylist and salon; that familiarity is a big reason they will keep coming back for more. From the moment they step through the door, try to keep a true vibe and a comfortable feel. Doing these things will make you the obvious choice to come back to.

5. Embrace the idea of your guests bringing inspirational photos to their appointments. A photo can give you a clear vision of what they are looking for in terms of cut, style, color, or type of updo. Photos are a great place to start because a picture will give you an idea of your guest's preferences, and then you can give them your professional opinion. You will need to mention in the conversation that no two heads of hair are alike. When looking at an inspirational photograph, consider how your client's hair compares to the model's in terms of texture, thickness, condition, length, fullness, fineness, and whether it is straight or curly. In other words, the picture should be used as a guide only.

6. Have a positive and sunny approach. Let yourself have fun and go with a natural flow. Keep an upbeat attitude so that clients will want to visit you and will look forward to their next appointment.

7. Keep grounded and healthy by taking good care of yourself. Go to the doctor and dentist for regular care. Go to the gym or yoga studio for your fitness. You will have a better disposition and feel great.

8. Think about what your next day's book looks like before you plan on partying. I have seen the effects when a stylist forgets to keep this in mind, and it is not pretty. If you don't think clients pick up on it too, well, you are wrong! Also, *never* go to the salon when you've been drinking. There are a boatload of reasons not to do this, safety being one of the biggest.

9. Be authentic. While our business is pleasing our clients in order to make them happy and encourage them to return, you should never try so hard to please that you end up being fake and not the real you. Clients will gravitate to you for what your authentic self has to offer, not some fake version. Who wants to put up a facade and constantly play that game? Be the natural you and wonderful clients will come.

10. Remember the importance of pre-booking. While your client is in your chair being serviced, you will want to talk with them about why it's important for them to come back every four to six weeks. You can explain that it will keep their color fresh and will keep their hair shaped nicely, at the perfect length. At the end of the appointment you should always ask if your client would like to re-book with you. Let your client know that in order for them to get the day and time of their choice they need to get in your schedule. Pre-booking will make your life easier too. You will know in advance what you have on your schedule, which will make it easier to prepare for your upcoming weeks.

11. Keep to your schedule. When you have an appointment scheduled, do everything that you can to be there for that service. Doing this will give your clients the peace of mind that comes with knowing you are a reliable stylist. All of us have things that come up—for example, sickness happens, and if you are really sick you should absolutely not go in. But if you are not going to make it into the salon, let your scheduled guests know as soon as possible, then try to get them back on your schedule as quickly as possible. If there is a client who really can't wait to be seen, offer them your first available

opening or have them see another stylist within your salon.

12. Don't be afraid to charge what you're worth! Being a stylist is unique in that you become very friendly with your clients, then feel as though you can't charge what you're worth. But this is your livelihood, and you need to make a living in spite of the fact that your clients may become your friends. This is especially important when you are a booth renter or suite or salon owner. You could risk losing your business if you don't charge what you should. Never feel badly about charging the appropriate amount for services or raising your prices. Keeping your prices competitive will allow you to structure your business around keeping your clients happy, while still being able to make a nice, comfortable living.

13. Find a financial adviser. A smart and savvy stylist understands the need for financial security. Find a good adviser that will help you reach your goals for the future. Whether you are just starting in the business or are a seasoned professional, the time to start is now!

Find an accountant you are comfortable with as well. They will be your guide to everything you need to know about doing your taxes, what you can claim as a stylist, and any other financial issues that you may have questions about. If you are an independent stylist, you will need to save your receipts for everything you buy for your business, as these are the items that you can claim. Stay as organized as possible and consider having a separate business checking account. Doing things this way will keep your home finances separate from your business.

14. Don't take it personally if a client leaves. You will have clients that will leave you. There are a number of reasons why this may happen: perhaps a client has moved, your hours, prices, or location don't suit them, or they simply decided a change may do them good. Don't fret! If it has been a while since you last saw a client, send them an email or a message. Tell them you've been thinking about them and offer them an incentive to come back, perhaps a percentage off a service or a free deep conditioner or eyebrow wax. You may or may not receive a response, but at this point you have done your part. Always stay positive and professional, and never think badly of a client who has left you, because you never know the reason they left or whether they will make their way back to you.

15. Always envision yourself sitting in your chair and think about how you would want to be treated

as a client. Your customer service needs to be on point, and then kicked up a notch. Show your clients the way it should be to have a service done by a caring stylist. Going above and beyond for your guests will make them happy and encourage them to come back to see you.

16. Remember that you are human and not perfect. There will be probably many times that you will make mistakes with your guests. Some will be small in nature, while others may be more monumental. In either case, it is best to own up to what has happened. The first step would be an apology for the incident and the extra time needed to resolve the issue. Your client will respect you for your honesty. Then you can give a basic explanation of what you intend to do to fix the problem. Next, you'll want to go above and beyond for your guest by offering them a free conditioning treatment, a free take-home product, or a percentage off their next service. This will make it clear to your client that you care about them and want to make it right. Your client will appreciate the effort, and in doing these things for them you will more than likely keep them as a future client.

17. Handle bad reviews the right way. You go online and OMG, a bad review pops up! Don't panic. (I

know, too late!) So what do you do if you get a bad online review? First of all, take a deep breath. This is not the end of the world. Take some time and don't respond right away, because if you do the words may not be what you really intend and you may come across as angry. Step away for a bit and really think about how to proceed. Firstly, stay professional and let the client know that you hear what they are saying. Most people want to be heard above all else. So make it known that you are listening to them and you'd like to take care of any issue they may have. Then you can simply ask if they would like to communicate with you privately, as it is generally better to get the conversation out of the public eye and to get more clarity on the issue. The more quickly you let them know that you hear them and you want to make things right, the more they will be inclined to speak with you directly to get the issue resolved. When you are speaking privately, let the client talk, and really listen. The problem may actually be a very easy one to fix. Ask them to come back into the salon so you can get a good look and figure out the best course of action. Do whatever you can to make things right.

A few things not to do: don't ignore the review, don't lash out at the person (this may feel right at first, but it is very unprofessional), don't get into a back-and-forth fight online, and don't delete the review (unless it is offensive or abusive, then by all means, delete!), because this will make them feel ignored and may lead to more bad reviews. Not only will lashing out or arguing not be helpful, but also, anyone reading it will get the impression that you are not handling the review appropriately.

18. While you are servicing a client, be aware of all the small details of the appointment. For instance, while shampooing a guest, do they say they love the smell? Let them know what you're using, why it's good for them, and that you have some for sale that they can use at home. While you are cutting a guest's hair, they may happen to mention that their hair gets frizzy or that they have some thinning areas that are of concern to them. This is the perfect opportunity to talk about shampoos, conditioners, or styling products that are designed to help with their specific needs. Or if you happen to notice that your client's eyebrows are in need of a shaping, let them know that you do facial waxing and would be happy to help them, if they like. Your client may not know that you do waxing, so here's your opportunity to let them know. It is truly all of these small cues that will get your clients what they need and keep you busy with all of your happy clients.

19. Reevaluate your work life whenever necessary. If the salon you are currently working in is not making you happy, then why stay? All of us make the best decisions possible based on what we know at the time. This means you may have started working in a salon that you thought you'd like, but over time, found that it doesn't feel quite right anymore. Maybe you are having an issue with a coworker or salon owner that can't be resolved, or dealing with an unprofessional atmosphere, a lack of walk-in clients, or a salon that is not in a good location. These are all valid reasons why you may want to make a change. If it doesn't seem like a fit for you anymore, and one or more of the problems I mentioned are resonating with you, it may be time to explore other options. It is an amazing feeling when you take that leap and realize that you are finally where you should be. Moving on from a salon that doesn't fit well in your life plan will be one of the best things that you can do for yourself and your clients. Yes, change can be scary, but it is also quite necessary if you are unhappy. So if that's the case, take some time to figure out what you need to do to take that next step and put yourself in a healthy salon. I can't stress to you enough that your happiness is what matters most, because when you are happy, clients will feel that good vibe and they will be happy to be with you.

20. Stay focused on your existing clients. It is easier to keep the clients you already have than to find and retain new ones, so it is very important to do what it takes to keep your clients as happy as you can. Finding new and interesting ideas for them and making new suggestions will help keep things fresh. Also, finding some new product lines will keep things interesting for your long-term guests, especially if they have been using the same line for a while. Making these little suggestions will keep the clients you already have coming back for more.

21. Use the best products available. Being a stylist means that you are upholding the professionalism of this industry, and clients walk through your door expecting a certain level of high-end products to be used on them and available for their at-home needs. This is why you should never buy low-end, non-professional brands for any of your lines. You should be using the best of what's available to you and never cut corners by using anything that is readily available to the public. This also goes for your tools, such as curling irons, straighteners, hair dryers, and even clippers and trimmers. Professional-grade products are well made and are more durable for constant use.

22. Never allow a guest to supply their own products. If a client brings their own products from home into your salon, do not use them. You are the professional, and you should be using only the products that you supply from your distributor. This applies to any kind of styling product, as well as perms or colors. This is important because you have no idea where these products came from or how old they are. The safety of your guest should be your number-one concern, and using a product that you have no knowledge of is very risky. Let your client know that if they want to be serviced by you, you will supply everything needed to do their hair professionally and with their safety in mind.

23. Don't be afraid to end a relationship that isn't working. You will have some clients come into your salon whom, for whatever reason, you are just not compatible with. This happens. Perhaps it is a personality issue and you just don't click, or maybe it comes down to a lack of communication, where you don't fully understand each other. Sometimes you may find that you can't seem to please the client, no matter what you do. If you see any of these issues arising and it's draining your energy, now is the time to do something about it. You will need to let your client know that although you've enjoyed

getting to know them and it's not an easy decision to make, you will no longer be able to service them. If they question you more about it, you could respond by saying, "I don't feel as though I can accommodate your needs anymore." Make sure at this point to have another stylist in mind and let the client know that this person will be a really nice fit for them. Make sure you have already spoken to your co-stylist and they are okay with that arrangement. Being professional throughout the whole process will make it easier on everyone, especially if you will be seeing them occasionally in the salon.

24. Find your passion to stay motivated. Do you love what you do as a stylist, or has it become "just a job"? Hopefully it is still your passion, but if not, this may be a good time to do some soul searching to figure out why. You may just need a bit of a push in the right direction, which can come from taking a class, going to a hair show, looking into new marketing techniques, or making and posting videos. Find your passion within the business by becoming an educator, a product representative, or a specialist in whatever comes naturally to you and whatever you are passionate about. Are you in love with doing formal hair? Perhaps you could become a bridal stylist. Do you work well with the elderly?

Nursing-care facilities generally have a salon and a few stylists working within them. Are you drawn to working with kids? There are salons that are specifically geared toward children that may be perfect for you. Basically, find what you are good at and what you like doing, then really hone in on that particular aspect. Don't ever feel like you have to spread yourself thin by being perfect at all things hair-related—our industry doesn't work like that. Putting too much pressure on yourself can cause you to feel overwhelmed and make you question being in the business. Finding your passion in the industry will make you realize you made a wonderful career choice.

25. Lastly, always be committed to the growth of your business. Keep up with the latest techniques, add beautiful finishing touches to your salon decor, be persistent when it comes to marketing yourself and your salon, and be a consistent stylist who is known for being reliable, honest, and caring. Doing these things will show that you love what you do and will help your business thrive.

QUESTION

What is the most significant idea from this chapter that you can implement in your day-to-day salon life?

_____

_____

_____

_____

_____

_____

_____

TIME TO REFLECT AND
TAKE THE CHALLENGE

In this chapter you learned a great deal about the fundamentals of being in the hair industry. Take two of these new ideas and work on setting your own goals to become better at the basics.

_____

_____

_____

_____

_____

_____

_____

CHAPTER 12
GOING INDEPENDENT

———

When you have been in the business for some time, have established yourself in the industry, and have built up a nice-sized clientele, you may want to consider becoming a more independent stylist. Being an independent stylist means that you do not work for the salon; you work within it, usually as a booth or suite renter. This allows you to make your own decisions when it comes to your clients and every other aspect of your career. You can set your schedule, your hours, what you charge, what hair products you provide, and what product lines you use. Being an independent stylist also means that you'll need to have a stellar website, a substantial social media presence, and really well-thought-out business cards, menus, and referral cards. You need to be willing to take the time to create a brand for yourself and your business. These aspects are all very important because you will be the one to market yourself and get new clients. Another thing to consider when going independent is that you will need to have your own liability insurance, whereas when you're employed at a salon, they hold the liability insurance for you. I've found that prices vary greatly from company to company, so do your research on lots of different insurance companies to get a good rate and the right coverage.

When deciding to go independent, finding the right salon situation will be key to your success and prosperity. When you find your salon home, it can make all the difference in the world in terms of your own happiness and the happiness of your guests. You will enjoy going to the salon because it won't feel like work; your clients will sense this joy and will enjoy coming to you, and in turn will send you more referrals. Doesn't this sound wonderful? Keep reading to find out if going independent is right for you.

BOOTH RENTING

Booth renting is when you pay rent to the owner of the salon for your own station. Typically your rent will cover your station, including a chair, mirror, and counter, the utilities, such as water, electric, heat, and air conditioning, and in some salons, wi-fi and beverages may also be included. The specifics of what is included would be outlined in your contract. Your personal cost would be for supplies such as colors, perms, combs, capes, scissors, hot tools, products to sell and use, towels, liability insurance, business cards and referral cards, and any advertising that you do. Becoming a booth renter is a great transition from hourly or commission-based salons. It allows you to be in charge of your own business, finances, and work station, providing the benefits of having your own business and making your own hours without the hassle of being a salon owner. Pricing your own services as you see fit is another added benefit. A must-have for any booth renter is a decent-sized clientele. You will need enough clients to be able to pay for all of your costs and still have money left over for yourself. If you are finding it hard to figure out whether this option would be financially beneficial for you, have an accountant look over all of your numbers. This is something that any savvy businessperson would do! Having some marketing knowledge is a plus, since you will be the one doing this for your business. If you don't know a lot on the subject, there are many books that you can read specifically about marketing, or you could listen to a podcast or speak to other stylists about how they have confidently marketed themselves.

SUITE RENTING

Another option is to rent a private suite located in a building with other like-minded businesses. In a suite rental, you would have a door with a lock and have the luxury of coming and going as you please. If you like being one-on-one with your guests, but still enjoy being around other stylists and beauty professionals, then this would be an ideal situation. Most suites will provide the basic equipment for you, such as mirrors, a stylist chair, a sink, and cabinets, which leaves you with the fun part—decorating your suite to suit your taste. Have a blast with this part and truly make it your own. Because this will be officially *your* salon suite, you'll need to come up with a name for your salon (how exciting!). As a suite renter you will be responsible for rent, business cards and menus, products, supplies, liability insurance, furniture (if not provided), decor, and all the marketing for your salon. Suite renting is a great idea if you want to have your own salon, but without the worry of having to maintain a full-sized salon. The lease you sign will give you all the details of what is covered in the rent and what would be expected of you. As with being a booth renter, being a suite renter means you need to know how to market yourself, have financial understanding, and have a nice-sized clientele.

OPENING UP A SALON

Are you a take-charge kind of person? Do you have business experience? Would you like to help other stylists succeed? Then owning a salon may be just what you're looking for. To take this step, you will need vast knowledge of the hair industry and a solid understanding of business management. You'll need to have a good financial plan in order, and to have an understanding of where the funds would be coming from to open the salon and how repayment will be made. Would you rent a space and build up the salon from scratch? The benefits of building up a salon from scratch are: You will be able to design the salon to suit your taste, you will pick the location, and everything within the salon would be fresh and new, which is good for clients and stylists alike. Would you purchase an existing salon? The benefits of purchasing an existing salon are: You will have everything needed when you start (if salon equipment is included), there may be stylists who were working at the previous salon that will work with you, and clients will easily find you, due to the fact that the salon is already established. There are benefits to both ideas.

When you become a salon owner, you are the one in charge of making all the decisions about the salon. You'll need to handle all aspects of the business, including hiring any employees or booth renters, making sure your lease is in order, marketing for a healthy business, buying all the necessary equipment and supplies (which can be a rather lengthy list), fixing all the things that need fixing, paying the rent and utilities, and taking care of any issues with your staff. You will choose the hours of operation, decide whether to provide in-salon education, decorate to suit the salon's vibe, and at times, will have to deal with unhappy staff and clients. You'll need to be available to your staff anytime, in case something arises that needs your attention. Opening a salon is a major undertaking, and for that reason it should be well thought out.

BUSINESS MENTORS

When you have gotten to this level and really want to amp up your presence, you may want to consider finding a salon coach or a business mentor. This person could be a successful industry friend, someone you find through an online community, or someone you hire. Finding the right coach or mentor will help to keep you motivated and move your career in a positive direction. They will coach you on what it takes to be successful and help you gain the confidence you need to maintain a flourishing business. Are you friendly with a successful salon owner? If so, why not sit with them over coffee and ask some questions? Another way to stay motivated would be to collaborate with a group of well-qualified, like-minded independent stylists or salon owners. This group will understand everything you are going through, so they will be able to give you good advice. What is the best way to find these like-minded individuals? Do a search on social media. There are groups that are specifically designed for people in the industry just like you. This is a fabulous way to give and get advice about marketing, client retention, product sales, new products, pricing issues, or anything else salon related. Sometimes all it takes is to start up a conversation with others in the industry to make great connections and learn so much.

WORKING WITH A DISTRIBUTOR

Going independent means that you will be responsible for buying your own products, including anything that you use on your guests. Make sure you keep an inventory of everything you have and what you use. This way you will be better prepared and will know what you need before you go to your distributor, and you'll avoid running out of stock.

A few tips when going to your distributor:

- Have a detailed list of everything you need, especially color. Keep track of what you've used and stock up.

- Make sure you get on the distributor's email list. This is how you will be notified about new products, classes, and sales.
- When they are having a sale, stock up! Buy the things you use most in bulk, such as products, colors, gloves, and bleach, to name a few. Some distributors will offer a percentage off the whole store, while others may have certain product lines on sale for certain days. This is one of the main reasons to subscribe to their email list, so you will know when your products are on sale.
- Sign up for rewards programs through all of your distributors.

While at your distributor, feel free to talk with the sales associates about any of their product lines. Since they come into contact with so many stylists on a daily basis, they will hear the most feedback about the lines they carry, including the good and the bad. Their knowledgeable recommendations can be a big help as you make your purchasing decisions.

IN CONCLUSION

In the thirty years I have been in the industry, I have worked at commission-based salons, worked independently as a booth renter, and finally opened up my own salon. For me, the biggest leap was when I went from working on commission to becoming a booth renter. I knew from that moment on that I was in charge of my career. This was a huge step for me, especially because I can struggle with change; something I'm sure some of you reading this will completely understand. Once I made that move and got going on my own, I immediately recognized that I had made the best decision for me. I was finally completely in charge of my career, and my confidence went through the roof. That newfound confidence made it easy for me to open up my salon (and write this book!), and I have never looked back.

Your journey will take you in whatever direction you choose, and as long as you are willing to embrace change, you will find the right salon. If you are fearful of change this can sound scary, but it's a necessary step in moving your career forward. Making small changes can give you the confidence you need to continue in the direction you want to go. The process of finding what fits for you cannot be rushed. When you take your time, breathe, and truly think about what it is that will make you happy, then you will find your answer. Enjoy the experiences along the way, and use them to gain the information needed to find exactly what it is you are looking for. Your happiness depends on it, and you are worth it!

QUESTION

Do you feel like becoming an independent stylist is for you? Write a list of the pros and cons of
going independent.

_____

_____

_____

_____

_____

TIME TO REFLECT AND
TAKE THE CHALLENGE

In this chapter you learned about the importance of
choosing the right salon situation. Close your eyes
and think about your ideal salon. Now, write down
everything that you envision. This can include the
size of the salon, its location, how it is decorated,
and whether it is a large booth rental salon with
coworkers, or a one-on-one salon suite. When you
finish your writing, do one thing every day that will
get you into that salon, using this list as your guide.

_____

_____

_____

_____

_____

**THANK YOU FOR TAKING THE TIME
TO READ *HAIR STYLIST VIBE*.**

Please consider leaving a review on Amazon.
All feedback is greatly appreciated.
Connect: hairstylistvibe@gmail.com
Facebook: Hair Stylist Vibe

MANY THANKS

———

I would like to thank my daughter, Christina, and my son, Bret, for supporting me through my journey with their absolute enthusiasm.

Kevin, for reading everything I threw his way, handling all of my computer woes, and being my rock!

My sisters, Holly and Laurie, my mom, my good friend Karen, and my entire family, for cheering me on every step of the way.

All of my wonderful clients, without whom this book would not exist. You all mean the world to me.

For making my book shine beyond my wildest dreams, I would like to thank my editor and proofreader, Christine McKnight, and my graphic designer, Danna Mathias.

Made in the USA
Monee, IL
12 May 2021

68398895R00095